- Excellence
- Doing Things the Right Way
- No Shortcuts
- Accountability

© 2023 Bertha Mae Publishing
ALL RIGHTS RESERVED

465 Nicollet Mall
Unit 2506
Minneapolis, MN 55401

info@mygreatauntedna.com

My Great Aunt EDNA: Excellence, **D**oing Things the Right Way, **N**o Shortcuts, & **A**ccountability

The Golden Girl of Leadership

Written by Mac McNeil

Edited by Peggy Downes

The views and opinions expressed in this book are my own, and they do not necessarily represent the views or opinions of my employers.

Table of Contents

1. Acknowledgements — 8
2. CHAPTER 1: My Auntie is Better Than Yours — 11
    a. My Great Aunt EDNA — 12
        I. Twin Souls
        II. Twice Born
        III. Personified
        IV. Results
    b. It Only Takes One — 16
        I. Setting Aunt EDNA's expectations
        II. Observations
        III. Trying to be Helpful
        IV. The Promotion
    c. Masculinity is a Prison — 17
        I. Engulfed in Bravado
        II. Copycat
        III. Observing & Admiring Leaders
        IV. Hermaphroditic Leadership
3. CHAPTER 2: Excellence — 20
    a. Excellence is a Spirit — 21
        I. Tell
        II. Show
        III. Celebrate
    b. Celebrity BootBLACK – What is Your Life's Blueprint? — 26
        I. Do that job so well
        II. Your own somebodiness
        III. Excellence in servant leadership
    c. All Around the World, Same Song — 30
        I. Emirates Airlines
        II. People thirst for leadership excellence
    d. The Spirit of Excellence Expects Opposition — 32
        I. The Counter-Spirit
        II. Weaponize
    e. Excellence – Confidence = Mediocrity — 34
        I. The Last Dragon
        II. Excellence = Mediocrity + Confidence

- f. Look for the Cracks — 37
  - I. Excellence born in abstruseness
  - II. What is a crack?
  - III. Inverse of light
- g. Playing the Wrong Chord Can Make Beautiful Music w/the Right Leader — 39
  - I. Jazz is King
  - II. Miles is the Master
  - III. Live Mistake
  - IV. 2 Seconds on the Mistake, 7 Seconds on Making it Right
- h. 29 Drops, 41 Tackles — 42
  - I. Excellence in job performance
  - II. Leadership shifts to ensure team success
  - III. Can a spirit be made?
- i. BFFs, Dudes, Homegirls, and Potnas — 42
  - I. Friend vs Friendly
  - II. Leading a Friend
- j. Sick & Tired of Being Sick & Tired — 46
  - I. Leader change
  - II. Team reconstructs
  - III. New vision
- k. Being Thankful for the Wilderness — 50
  - I. Slow & methodical occurrence
  - II. Leadership is lonely
  - III. Self-doubt
  - IV. Reflection & redirection
4. CHAPTER 3: Doing Things the Right Way — 54
   - a. Superglue Superheroes — 55
     - I. To the rescue
     - II. Partnership
   - b. Coach George — 57
     - I. Hit the hole
     - II. Same play, different results
     - III. Kid vs Adult

- c. And to this Plan, I Thee Wed — 61
  - I. Audible vows
  - II. Doing the right things vs. Doing Things the Right Way
  - III. Adaptation
- d. Communication is the Key & the Lock — 63
  - I. We all say stupid things
  - II. Withholding is the lock
  - III. Communicate how to do it
- e. The Law of Diminishing Returns — 67
  - I. Overutilization
  - II. Measuring marginal increase
  - III. Input variables must change
- f. Betting on Myself — 70
  - I. Pete Rose
  - II. What is leadership narcissism?
  - III. Iteration, evolution, and inherent risk

5. CHAPTER 4: No Shortcuts — 74
   - a. Baby, Don't Rush — 75
     - I. Jam on repeat
     - II. Wrong leadership map
     - III. Take the long way around
   - b. Which is Heavier, Money or People? — 77
     - I. Inspire or make money
     - II. Zero-gravity

6. CHAPTER 5: Accountability — 80
   - a. Accountability is Caring — 81
     - I. Mommy issues
     - II. You're part of the problem
     - III. Demonstrated care
   - b. I Did Not Ask for This — 84
     - I. Voluntold
     - II. Realistic expectations
   - c. Four Uses for Your Leadership Thumbs — 86
     - I. Pointing them at yourself
     - II. Hitchhiking

- III. Creating space
- IV. Recognition
- d. Broken Mirror — 92
  - I. Reflection vs. looking in a mirror
  - II. Segmented leadership face
- e. It Wasn't Me! — 94
  - I. Deny, deny, deny
  - II. Accountability list
- f. Still Waters Turn Green — 98
  - I. Stagnation invites unwanted guests
  - II. Leaders as pumps
7. My Inner Thoughts on Writing this Book — 100
8. Leader Bios — 102
9. About the Author — 116

ACKNOWLEDGEMENTS

I must first, and always, acknowledge God and my Savior Jesus Christ for leading me on this journey of life, placing me in the bloodline of Bertha Mae (Mays) Young and Edna Mae (Mays) Jeter, and directing my steps to arrive at the delivery of these words in book form. He used all of the steps of my life, including the ones where I tried to walk away from Him, to compile the story that I humbly invite you to read.

I acknowledge my mother, Cliffie (Cherri) Hatton, who at fifteen years of age gave birth to me and prayed me into what I am today. My mother was my first teacher of My Great Aunt EDNA principles before I even formulated the concept. She taught me to read and do math when I was three years of age, before ever stepping foot into pre-school. I was always ahead of my peer group because of the level of Excellence that she taught me. For me, my sister Pamela McNeil, and brother Demetrius McNeil, excelling was normal.

I acknowledge my father, Napoleon McNeil, Jr., who adopted me as his own when I was only three months old and displayed through daily and proper mannerisms of a real man as to how I should act. He was a quiet man as a father, but when he spoke, I knew it was important for me to listen and learn. His lessons will never be forgotten; both the spoken and unspoken lessons of a father. He was my first example of "what could be" walked out. He had a fourth-grade education when he joined the Army at age twenty-four, and by the time he passed, he had two Master's degrees. I remember tutoring him on basic math when I was eight years old so that he could get his GED, and he tutored me on life in return. It was a deal that benefited us both.

I acknowledge my birth father, Ernest Isom, who developed a loving relationship with me when I was twenty-seven years of age. In the five years that we truly spent together, my father taught me that distance is sometimes required in love. I did not understand this concept until we had our first man-to-man conversation. During this conversation, he praised my father Napoleon McNeil, Jr. and thanked him for how he raised me. He also stated that although he had to love me from afar for a while, he knew that his absence allowed the full family dynamic to develop in which I grew up in. However, he never stopped loving me, or secretly checking on my life. This lesson of leadership awareness and willingness to step down to allow another leader to step in for the good of the team will be discussed in this book. It came from him.

I acknowledge my wife, Cynthia McNeil, who quietly encourages me to continue to walk out my gifts. She has endured multiple relocations, cultural changes, and versions of me. She has seen in real-time the development of this leadership philosophy into what it is today. She has listened to multiple rants and fits about my workday, provided counsel, and has shared in many of the celebratory results from the fruit of the challenges overcome. She is the strongest woman I know, and I envy her power to unknowingly inspire others through her everyday journey.

I acknowledge my children, Shayna, Ashley, Simon, and Isaiah who had to endure the teachings of My Great Aunt EDNA as they grew up (still do at times). My children are the living examples that I truly believe and instill the principles of Excellence, Doing Things the Right Way, No Shortcuts, and Accountability. They can tell much better stories than I can, which would likely cause laughter and possibly instill fear in the listeners. But their successful lives are the results of these principles. I am so very proud of all four of them, and I am sure their children will learn of My Great Aunt EDNA as well.

I acknowledge Mrs. Claire Floto Billings, who was my AP English Teacher in the 11th grade in Fulda, Germany. Mrs. Floto (as I know her) was the first teacher to instill in me the love for reading and writing in a structured, yet interesting format. Through various beatings, yelling, C- papers, and pure classroom humiliation (I'm seriously joking), she instilled a life-long love of the written word in me and several others at Fulda American High School. She was a gentle teacher, who had a soft voice, which was authoritative and sensitive, simultaneously. I do not remember all of my teachers, but I will never forget Mrs. Floto.

I acknowledge all of the leaders who have contributed to the formulation of My Great Aunt EDNA's framework, especially to those who directly contributed to this book via interview or written contribution. I have had the great pleasure of working with some amazing business leaders whom, very much like my experience with my father, I observed and mimicked. Dr. Claude T. Williams, Barbara (Tripp) Milazzo, Coach Marcus George, LTC (Ret.) Shaun Lott, Billy Taylor, Pablo Sanchez, Maria Garcia, Brian Giles, Patrick Clooney, Al Arguello, Vera Stewart, Deirdre Allen, Ron Everett, Samantha Melting, and Kurt Grossheim are just a few of the names of leaders from whom I have learned so much from. My Great Aunt EDNA would not be a book without them.

I need to acknowledge ALL of the great teams I have led who have embraced and personified My Great Aunt EDNA in your work performance and lives! If it were not for you all (wish I could name all of the thousands of you) My Great Aunt EDNA would have never become a leadership philosophy with proven results.

I love you all. - Mac

TECHNICAL ACKNOWLEDGEMENTS

- Book Cover Jamie Ty
  https://www.100covers.com

- Book Editing Peggy Downes
  piggelyd@gmail.com

- Content Strategy Coach Raza Imam
  https://www.authorpreneurelite.com/

- Digital Marketing Kazi Giysuddin
  https://www.kazimarketing.com

- Podcast Booking Daniel Gefen
  https://gefenmediagroup.com/

- Signature Logo
  https://www.artlogo.co

- YouTube Show Video Editing Everritt Edwards
  visualsbyevpro@gmail.com

Chapter 1: MY AUNTIE IS BETTER THAN YOURS

- Excellence
- Doing Things the Right Way
- No Shortcuts
- Accountability

My Great Aunt EDNA

I really do have a Great Aunt Edna. She was the twin of my grandmother Bertha Mae (Mays) Young, both born on October 26, 1933, in Mississippi. Although she and I had little interaction in my lifetime, her persona has helped to shape my career and thousands of others unbeknownst to her. In fact, she is somewhat of a celebrity in the teams whom I have led over my career, both large and small. My Great Aunt EDNA started out as an acronym I stumbled upon when someone asked me what made me a successful leader. The question caused me to ponder and reflect on the common characteristics of the teams that I have led. In a brief, yet impactful moment of response, I stated, "**Excellence, Doing Things the Right Way, No Shortcuts, and Accountability**." And just like that, my Great Aunt EDNA was born for the second time.

From the mouths of her own daughters, Debra, Brenda, and Karen, Edna Mae (Mays) Jeter had the biggest heart ever. She had a heart of gold. She loved her family dearly and it showed. There was always a meal ready, or one being prepared, and anyone who walked through the door was welcome to partake. For those who needed feeding and couldn't come to her, she took it to them. She was Aunt Edna to everybody.

If you asked the many people that were around her for any length of time, they would talk about how she lived her faith. If you talked to any of the many people that walked through the doors of her home, they would talk about how she loved and cared for others. Her love embodied everything about her. A relative recently referred to her home as the central hub or safe haven for anybody who needed a place to rest, reset, and/or recoup. This was, in large part, due to the emphasis that both Edna and William Jeter placed on family.

Those who needed refuge or care knew they could find it at her home. It didn't matter who...nieces, nephews, cousins, aunts, uncles, parents, blood relatives from both families, relatives by marriage, whomever. She loved everybody. Her strength, fairness, compassion, and love were amazing. Whether it was for a few days, a few weeks, months, and yes, sometimes years, their home had revolving doors. You were welcome once, twice, and time and time again.

Even in a small house, somehow there was always room for just one more, and it never seemed crowded. With the exception of her father, who passed away before Edna Mae married, both sets of parents lived with them at some point. There were extended family members who spent time under their roof and to this day they are still considered to be "family." Edna made everyone feel special. Whether it was a pillow to lay one's head, a savory home cooked meal, or a caregiver until...whenever. She opened her doors; she opened her arms...she opened her heart. She poured out love.

My Aunt Edna was a firm believer in doing right. She believed doing right was the easiest thing to do. If something felt wrong or if you had to question whether it was right or wrong, you just didn't do it. She believed everything you do should be given your best effort, and your best effort is always right. She never asked us to be perfect, but she always expected our best. That's how she lived...a standard of best, and it showed in everything she did.

Nothing went undone, and no one was neglected. Her cooking was legendary. Everyone coveted an invite to dinner. If you asked the many people who she cooked for over the years, they would brag on her culinary skills. Every day, there was a cooked meal, except most Fridays. Friday was our day to make tacos, or fish sticks, or get fast food somewhere, which we thought was a huge deal. Sundays were like going to a restaurant for a 3-course meal.

My Aunt Edna sewed like a trained tailor. She often made our clothes, which looked just as good, or better than the ones we picked from the Sears catalogue at the start of each school year. While working full time and being a caregiver to many, she made being a wife and mother of four look easy. She poured her love for family and life into everyone.

Over the years, my teams have taken it upon themselves to personify my Great Aunt EDNA in various ways, including the production of large caricatures of her placed in break rooms, conference rooms, and PowerPoint presentations. I have even received heartwarming emails from leaders who I have helped develop, and who have moved on to greater things, tell me stories of how My Great Aunt EDNA has helped their teams achieve greatness or overcome obstacles. Those moments always make me smile, and I feel a sense of pride in knowing they actually listened to her throughout their time of interacting with me as their leader.

The real secret of My Great Aunt EDNA is not in the cuteness of the personification (although she is very cute), nor the ease of slipping her into a coaching session with a team member, but in what she represents. My Great Aunt EDNA represents an important ingredient in the culture in which my teams operate. She sets the standard in all our interactions. In fairness of clarity, she is not judgmental in her delivery of the message, but stern in her seriousness of the expectations (very much like my grandmother and the real Great Aunt Edna).

It Only Takes One

My Great Aunt EDNA's personification is legendary. The conceptual congregation of her attributes are by no means revolutionary in themselves, however, when the culture is collectively achieved, the results, attitudes, and life-lessons learned are undeniable.

It only takes one brave soul on the team to adopt My Great Aunt EDNA to ignite a true cultural paradigm shift. I purposefully utilize the word "adopt," because simply being introduced to My Great Aunt EDNA will not accomplish the results the team needs to achieve results beyond standard beliefs. I very vividly recall being tasked as a VP, Operations Market Manager for a major bank to lead 60 Financial Centers and 72 managers reporting directly to me. These Financial Centers had mixed results in the previous year, and My Great Aunt EDNA was nowhere to be found.

After months of introducing My Great Aunt EDNA to the leadership team in this market, I began having direct meetings with their subordinate employees to measure the level of adoption of My Great Aunt EDNA. While at a Financial Center in the morning prior to opening, I thought I was helping by performing an "opening" duty that was observed by one of the Tellers. The Teller kindly yet firmly interrupted me in the middle of performing this task and stated, "Mac, we don't half-do anything at this center. Let me show you how to do this correctly." She proceeded to perform the task with a spirit of Excellence, and even led a brief coaching session with me on the importance of Doing Things the Right Way. Mind you, I was four levels above her in hierarchy and that didn't faze her one bit. At that moment, I knew My Great Aunt EDNA was beginning to take root on our team. I promoted her, and the market ended up finishing the year second in the country in performance out of 375 markets.

Although many people consider LeBron James to be a controversial figure, it is undeniable his approach to leadership is a successful reflection of My Great Aunt EDNA. LeBron James voluntarily returned to the Cleveland Cavaliers, who had the worst record in the NBA the previous year, and then won an NBA Championship the very next year. His presence, along with My Great Aunt EDNA in the spirit of Excellence, Doing Things the Right Way, No Shortcuts, and Accountability was all that was necessary for an entire organization to achieve what was initially considered impossible; it only takes one.

If you're a leader who strives to instill sustainable greatness in your team or organization, I challenge you to incorporate My Great Aunt EDNA into your culture. Observe, learn, and recognize the "one" that will ignite the culture for the rest of the organization. They just need an introduction to my Aunt.

Masculinity is a Prison

It was a beautiful evening on August 5, 2022, in Minneapolis, MN. The sun was still shining at 7:00 PM, and the temperature was a beautiful 80 degrees. I was walking north on Nicollet Mall near 8th Street, when a person walked by me wearing a t-shirt that boldly read, "Masculinity is a Prison." The message was an obvious shout out to LGBTQ+, and the eclectic attire of the person wearing the shirt fit right into Minneapolis' diverse population. I immediately began to ponder the message, and of course my mind led me to leadership and My Great Aunt EDNA.

My indoctrination into leadership was one of full-throttle male bravado. I was a Special Operations Command (Airborne) soldier, Military Intelligence Analyst, and am a Desert Storm veteran. The normal presence of leadership I was introduced to at the age of 17 included autocratic formality, profanity (still possess some of that), show of strength, and tales of grotesque encounters. I loved every bit of it! I can still recall the names of my Drill Sergeants with whom I only spent 2 months, but I struggle to remember the names of my direct supervisors over four years in civilian life. And now, I teach leadership principles in the persona of a feminine character named My Great Aunt EDNA. What a paradox, right? Not really. Let me explain my evolution.

Upon my release from the United States Army, into the shark-infested waters of civilian life, I began my junior leadership career. As a child learns to speak and act by mimicking, I mimicked the leadership styles of the masculine leaders of my past (both male and female). I was not successful, and the experiences left me confused. Why had others been "successful" with this leadership approach, and I was not? I immediately began to make up excuses that sounded something (or exactly) like, "It is because I am black. It is because I am young." You may be stating phrases like, "It is because I am a woman." "It is because I am gay." None of these statements are accurate. The truth is that unbridled masculinity in leadership is a prison. It is not only a prison for the team you lead, but also a prison for you as a leader, which causes you to believe that being "soft" as a leader leads you to failure.

I had the great pleasure of working for great leaders at JPMorgan Chase who helped reshape my thinking about leadership philosophies. One was a man, and two were women. What I noticed in the male leader was that "on stage" he carried a charismatic, boisterous, inspirational, and masculine tone that everyone in the room responded to quickly; very similar to the Drill Sergeants who I admired. However, when I had the opportunity to witness him "off-stage" with others, he was polite, considerate, attentive, and even soft-hearted in his leadership decision-making. The women leaders (whom I strongly admire to this day) were funny, down-to-earth, personable, and inspirational when in public settings. Yet, when I was able to witness them in settings with smaller audiences, they were direct, confident, smart, and definitive in their leadership decisions. These leaders helped me to understand that in leadership, masculinity that is unbalanced with feminism is a prison.

My Great Aunt EDNA is a combination of masculine and feminine characteristics. It is a hermaphroditic leadership approach. Prior to My Great Aunt EDNA, the only other hermaphrodite that garnered the attention and respect of the world that I was aware of was Prince! My Great Aunt EDNA is a sweet "old" lady, and my teams love to personify her in cute and comedic ways to have fun with her. It makes everyone on the team happy to share in the pleasure of being nieces and nephews of My Great Aunt EDNA. But don't get it twisted. My Great Aunt EDNA will get on your ass when necessary, and if she says the conversation is over, the conversation is over. The reason My Great Aunt EDNA has been so successful over the years is because she possesses both masculine and feminine characteristics. One without the other would not work. To achieve team culture of Excellence, Doing Things the Right Way, No Shortcuts, and Accountability, leaders need to understand this principle. I would only insert one small word in the t-shirt message reminding me of this principle. "Masculinity **Alone** is a Prison."

Chapter 2: EXCELLENCE

- Excellence
- Doing Things the Right Way
- No Shortcuts
- Accountability

Excellence is a Spirit

Excellence is a spirit, and as with all spirits, when it is present it is often not realized by those void of the spiritual vision to see it. Scales of mediocrity can cover and cloud the eyes of those sleepwalking in the trance of "good," to the point that excellence is unnoticed. Mediocrity is like a cloud that lingers too long on a partly cloudy day, which has sunshine in the afternoon forecast. Everyone is expecting the cloud to lift eventually, but when it does not, you simply go on with your day. If you live in Seattle, you get used to the fact that the cloud is virtually permanent, and when the sun actually does show up, it feels like a holiday. This is what happens when the spirit of Excellence shows up in situations where a cloud of mediocrity has become the norm. It shines so brightly that it may harm the eyes of those who have not adjusted.

I had a recent experience when I knew I was sitting next to Excellence personified. Her physical appearance was very much like the rest of the humans on the plane, but her aura was quite apparent, different and very bright. The conversation was initiated very similarly to the ones that begin with the person sitting next to you on the plane who you are hoping is not a weirdo, but it ended with a light that surrounded us, which I knew was orchestrated by something greater than the both of us. Her name is Nicole Tinson, and she is the Founder & CEO of HBCU 20x20. I did not know it initially when the conversation began, but Nicole is on the Forbes 30 Under 30 Social Entrepreneurs List. Once we got beyond the normal plane conversation regarding geographic destinations and why, we both realized that we had complimentary purposes. We both identify and exalt Excellence as a passion.

During a later interview I conducted with Nicole, she used a phrase I will not likely forget. She stated, "In my business of connecting talented HBCU graduates with corporate opportunities across the country, I have no choice but to operate in Excellence! Anything less will result in me being out of business." My Great Aunt EDNA expresses that Excellence is a spirit, but the choice of operating within that spirit is solely left up to the individual.

However, the worst-case scenario for a leader who seeks to instill My Great Aunt EDNA into their culture is when, similar to other spirits, the possibility of its existence is questioned. So how is a leader supposed to approach the challenges of vision and belief and create a team culture that is founded in the spirit of excellence? My Great Aunt EDNA has always instructed me to TELL, SHOW, and CELEBRATE.

- ❖ <u>Tell</u>

I frequently utilize storytelling from personal experiences to provide examples of Aunt EDNA in action, noting the results and challenges along the way. Not only are personal stories enticing to the eager ear, but adjacent stories involving others in action demonstrating the spirit of excellence are also impactful. I often use The Death Crawl scene from the movie **Facing the Giants** to illustrate the spirit of Excellence in leadership to the new teams I lead. I think I cry every time that I see this scene because of my passion for leadership and excellence. Leaders of My Great Aunt EDNA can utilize the same methodology in helping to dispel disbelief in cultural excellence entering their teams. Tell frequently, tell truthfully, and tell yourself.

One does not have to be an expert storyteller to be effective in introducing the importance of the spirit of excellence. The delivery of the story is not as impactful as the story points themselves. Some leaders are natural storytellers and can entice the suspenseful excitement in their listeners to hang on every word, while others can only tell you the beginning, middle, and the end of the story. Although one approach may be more fun, both versions of the story will drive impact.

I have often been surprised by the memory recall that a former employee displays to me when they tell me about a story I shared with them, which to be totally honest, I sometimes only vaguely remember. I have seen excitement and passion on their faces as they regurgitate the story back to me, while I am secretly trying to remember the details while smiling and nodding. Words are the most powerful tool on this planet. It would behoove all leaders to share them and tell the stories that helped to shape who they are.

❖ Show

Showing sounds self-explanatory, but showing requires action on the part of the leader. Simply telling your team about the spirit of excellence is not enough. As a reminder, excellence is a spirit, not a result. Many new leaders fail to implement *showing* into their cultural introduction of My Great Aunt EDNA because they feel they do not have viable or quantitative results to display for their teams. Excellence is displayed in the *how*, not the *what*. Simply take a task, preferably a small but important one, and allow the team to observe you doing it. There is no need to prelude their need to watch but make it convenient for them to do so. Be meticulous and purposeful in your actions, and do not make a big deal about the completion of the task or the results. Make a big deal in *how* the task was approached and implemented.

I know Missouri has laid claim to being the "Show Me" state, but I would suggest that this is a general sentiment of all cynical humans (about 99% of the human population). Most people will not buy in to a new philosophy, practice, or discipline without someone showing them what it is in actuality. Very similar to storytelling, the leader does not necessarily have to be the expert in the execution of the task shown. This "expert" mentality is what keeps some leaders from ever attempting to show a task; but take it from someone who has NEVER been the expert, do it anyway. The team needs to see it in action, and once they do, they will imagine and develop the excellence necessary to improve on your performance.

❖ <u>Celebrate</u>

My Great Aunt EDNA would like to begin this section by differentiating between recognition and celebration. Being recognized by your leaders and peers is a common (or should be) activity within most organizations to acknowledge positive behaviors and results. It usually involves written or verbal recognition, with a possible reward of some kind attached to the recognition. Recognitions come and go, and I think of them in the same way that I do a 3-Star restaurant; it was good, but I can't remember the name of the server.

But a celebration?! Now that is something memorable! I would like to challenge all of you reading this right now to think back to the first celebration of **you**, you can recall. Although the percentage might not be 100% of you, I would presume the event most of you recall occurred before your tenth birthday. Celebrations have a memory impact that is equivalent to trauma. They are implanted into our brains and hearts and impact our future actions and reactions. Therefore, My Great Aunt EDNA instructs leaders to celebrate the spirit of excellence in action. Your reward will be your teams' response by repeating behaviors that demonstrate the spirit of excellence. Eventually, anything less will be called out by the team, even if the inferior behavior is demonstrated by the leader.

One of the best corporate examples I have ever witnessed pertaining to truly celebrating the spirit of Excellence in operation is from JPMorgan Chase. When Chase celebrates, Chase celebrates! It is not a "Break out the paper plates, an iPhone, and a Spotify playlist" type of moment. It is a "Let us fly all of these Excellent employees and their spouses to the Atlantis Hotel in the Bahamas, all expenses paid for a week. And while we're at it, let's throw an evening beach party with exquisite food, beverages, and servants. And just for fun, let's give them a day when they can choose their own excursions at our expense." That actually happened, and trust me, this is the very definition of implanting a memorable moment into the brains and hearts of those celebrated. The natural human response is to want to replicate your efforts of Excellence to be able to experience it again. The spirit of Excellence will not easily dissipate in that type of environment.

Celebrity BootBLACK – What is Your Life's Blueprint?

"When you discover what you are going to be in life, set out to do it as if God almighty called you at this particular moment in history to do it. Do that job so well that the living, the dead, or the unborn couldn't do it any better. Sweep streets like Michelangelo painted pictures. Sweep streets like Beethoven composed music. Sweep streets like Leontyne Price sings before the Metropolitan Opera. Sweep streets like Shakespeare wrote poetry. Sweep streets so well that all the hosts of Heaven and Earth will have to pause and say, 'here lives a great street-sweeper who swept his job well'. " – Dr. Martin Luther King, Jr. I was reminded of this statement by one of the wisest men I have had the opportunity to interact with in a great while. I was in Washington, DC for a speaking engagement for the Jobs for America's Graduates 40th Anniversary Gala Event, held at the Hyatt Regency Washington on Capitol Hill. While still in my room early in the day, I looked at my light brown Allen Edmonds shoes and said to myself, "Wow, these babies need a good shine." I proceeded down to the lobby to grab some overpriced coffee, and lo and behold, a smiling and handsome brotha was standing next to a shoeshine business I was unaware existed in the hotel. I smiled back and stated, "I'm coming to see you next, sir."

With my highly overpriced caramel macchiato in hand, I headed to the chair and stepped up to be assisted. This gentlemen immediately said, "Those are Allen Edmonds" from sight alone. "*Impressive*," I thought. What I learned in the next thirty minutes made that one impressive act look small. I was introduced to Mr. Dino Wright, founder, and shoeshine extraordinaire of Celebrity BootBlack, LLC. His spirit exuded joy, and he made my blasé morning become one of insightful reflection, watching videos of Dr. Martin Luther King, Jr. and Leontyne Price, and fate contemplation. Dino informed me that he had been at that hotel site for forty-three years as a shoeshine expert. He was originally from Buffalo, NY, but made his way to Washington D.C. for college, just after Ronald Reagan was announced as President of the United States. He recalls his parents stating, "Son, we did not send you to Washington D.C to shine shoes." He replied, "I want to make my own money," and he saw the opportunity the new California "immigrants" would allow for anyone who provided great service and a spirit of Excellence.

He recalled a speech that Dr. Martin Luther King gave, in which Dr. King encouraged his attentive audience, "Your life's blueprint should include a basic principle, a determination to achieve Excellence in your various fields of endeavors. It should include a deep belief in your own dignity, your own worth, and your own somebodiness." (Dr. Martin Luther King, "What is Your Life Blueprint?"). Mr. Wright took that statement and ran with it in his soul to produce a lucrative shoeshine and coat-check business with five locations in the metropolitan Washington D.C. area. Via osmosis, one can feel his sense of pride and joy in what he does for a living, and the difference he makes in the lives of those "immigrants" passing through D.C. for whatever reason.

I am thankful for my 30 minutes of wisdom from Mr. Wright, as he reminded me leadership does not only exist in the form of a hierarchical structure, but it lives in the moment of self-worth, and as Dr. King said, "somebodiness." As you begin to KNOW and flow in who you are with a spirit of Excellence, you immediately pick up the mantle of leadership whether you want it or not. People are observing you in how you lead YOU! Do you lead you by operating in Excellence, Doing Things the Right Way, taking No Shortcuts, and holding yourself Accountable? Mr. Wright never once mentioned to me, "I am a leader in my field." He did not have to. I saw it in how his spirit spoke through his work and his smile. I knew it by the humility and pride he took in making a stranger feel better about myself as I walked away from his business knowing others would admire my shoes, thus adding to my own self confidence.

At the event, I met several leaders with big titles such as Governor, Chief Executive Officer, Chief Operations Officer, Senior Vice President of blah, blah, blah. I even have one of those blah, blah, blah titles myself. It is not easy to lead in any of those roles, but those roles are no more important nor impactful than a leadership role in shining shoes in a premier hotel in one of the most important cities in the world. I would even suggest Mr. Wright has more influence and opportunities to encourage and influence leaders than any of the aforementioned titles. People of all statures let their guards down in his cold-attitude-melting smile. They tell Mr. Wright secrets they would not share with their own executive peers. They ask Mr. Wright for advice in multiple matters of life that they would not ask their executive assistants. He, and other "servant-leaders" operating in My Great Aunt EDNA's culture never make the Wall Street Journal but are, by every definition of the word, leaders.

At the same event, I had the opportunity to present and speak to 250 young leaders from 39 states across the country representing Jobs for America's Graduates. One of the questions I received from the audience was pertaining to career path and how they should begin to prepare for their own. I responded that a true career path is never a straight line, and they should experience as many quirky opportunities that present themselves. I hope a few of them read this, as Mr. Wright is a perfect example of what I was attempting to relay in my response. Mr. Wright is a college-educated man who chose to veer from his original plan to become a servant leader. His life's accumulation of experiences, wealth, and world travel is comparable to the blah, blah, blah titles aforementioned, but it is only because of the spirit of Excellence he carries pertaining to his somebodiness. My Great Aunt EDNA would appreciate and admire the Life Blueprint that Mr. Wright laid out for others to study.

All Around the World, Same Song

For those of you who are not hip-hop heads from the 80's and 90's like me, this sub-title is a shout out to Digital Underground (featuring 2Pac), and their song that explains that things are always the same around the world. As Proverbs in the Bible states, "There is nothing new under the Sun." I write this as I fly on Emirates Airlines across Europe on my way to Dubai, UAE, with Chennai, India as a final destination. We now venture into the world beyond corporate American leadership, and into worldview philosophies derived from personal interactions with individuals who have real-life, globally-lived experiences. On this flight alone, I have had the great pleasure of speaking with a white businessman from Belgium whose work focuses on minority inclusion for women beyond the United States, a white male flight attendant from Northern Spain, who admittedly had limited access to other nationalities prior to joining Emirate Airlines, a black male flight attendant from Costa Del Sol Spain of Portuguese descent, and a white female Polish bartender who grew up in post-Soviet Union Europe and shuns all philosophies of former-times Eastern Europe. This is the very definition of diversity, all on one flight.

As I had marvelous conversations with them all (I'm a social butterfly), I asked them all the same question: "Why Emirates Airlines?" Regardless of the mind-wondering adventures, concepts, and historical frame of references they shared in their colorful stories, they all answered this question the same: "It's the best." Of course, my own observations illuminated this truth, but I wanted to ask why they chose what they deemed to be the best prior to ever experiencing it themselves. The flight attendants answered, "I had plenty of choices, but the lure of Emirates and the fact that it is based in Dubai was an easy choice." The passengers answered, "I had flown other airlines internationally, but had always heard of the excellence of Emirates, and I wanted to see it for myself."

So, what do I deduce from these pricked responses? I deduce that Excellence is universal, as much as it is infectious. All people are attracted to Excellence, and they typically hear the story of excellence prior to ever experiencing it. Once someone is "infected" with Excellence, mediocrity immediately becomes an environment with which they no longer want to be associated. In considering leadership in this conversation, leaders who can "infect" their team with Excellence can create impact beyond their immediate circle of influence. However, the task is not an easy one.

My Great Aunt Edna used to tell me, "Baby, it is easier to pull ten donkeys up a steep mountain in the snow with one rope, than it is to pull one human up the same mountain who doubts that you can." The leadership challenge is to get one human to believe that you can, and then allow you to do it. I think of the beginning of Emirate Airlines. I am sure there were people around the world who doubted that a middle Eastern country, which was little more than one street and dust in 1980, could become the most sought-after airline flight routes in the world. Yet, it was accomplished with leadership belief, and the ability to block out naysayers.

General leadership is the same. It takes one or two leaders to come together to say, "we can," make the tough choices to eliminate mediocre thought processes, and act on Excellence every day. Excellence asks, "What is better than the current best?" "What hasn't the current best considered?" Excellence is not concerned with the cost, because it understands that all people are willing to pay for excellence when it is presented and the means to pay exists. All around the world, people seek out leaders who embody and live out these principles. They thirst for it; literally. Many will walk hundreds of miles to get to that "world," and others die trying to reach it. ¿Porque?

The answer is because Excellence is authentic. All else is bullshit in various forms. The greatest compliment a leader can receive is to have people want to work with them in multiple organizations or situations. It typically has very little to do with personality comfortability. It is because one recognizes a particular leader will observe, deduce, make changes, and create environments of Excellence in which to operate. Excellence is just a more comfortable flow. As a reminder, Excellence is not perfection. It is the spirit and intent in the way teams move.

As I sit in the Dubai airport, I wish I had the opportunity to speak with the initial leadership team who dreamed up the next level of Excellence in air travel. I would have liked to have heard the debates, read the written visions, and understood their plan of execution to arrive at where they are today. All I can do is imagine and admire, just as a nephew of My Great Aunt EDNA should.

The Spirit of Excellence Expects Opposition

Every spirit has a counter-spirit. The spirit of happiness has a counter spirit of sadness. The spirit of racism has a counter spirit of unity. The counter spirit of excellence is mediocrity. Many would argue that excellence has many *opposites* other than mediocrity; true. However, the **counter-spirit** of excellence is mediocrity. Remember, excellence is determined in the *how*, and not the result. Mediocrity in itself can be very comfortable for many souls. Millions of people every day go home with a smile in their hearts leaving environments of mediocrity that do not bother them one bit. However, when the spirit of excellence presents itself in their safe spaces of mediocrity, situations can become very tense, very quickly. Why? The answer is because when a spirit is confronted by its counter, conflict is inevitable.

Leaders who newly adopt My Great Aunt EDNA into their team culture must be prepared for conflict. Conflicts require weaponry, but my Great Aunt EDNA does not equip her leaders with everyday weapons. Oh no! The weapons handed down to me by My Great Aunt EDNA are not for the faint of heart. They are not for the quick-tempered. They are not for the impatient. As she once told me, "Either you learn to become patient, or you become a patient." They are not for the judgmental. "Judges already have a job, and you don't look good in a robe." These weapons will test the very being you initially believed yourself to be. The weapons to confront the spirit of mediocrity supplied by My Great Aunt EDNA are personal connectivity, listening, empathy, humanization, laughter, silliness (yes, I said silliness), and constant reminders that mediocrity will not be celebrated.

So, how do you "weaponize" personal connectivity in order to confront mediocrity, you ask? In any conflict, physical or mental, a wall of protection is immediately formed by the opponent as a method of protecting one's body, pride, or in this case, comfort. The wall, although invisible to most, is designed to not allow the opponent to penetrate or harm what is being protected. In the case of comfort, conscious and subconscious means will be deployed to either disprove the possibility of excellence being achieved in their environment, or disproving/dishonoring the messenger of My Great Aunt EDNA.

By working to create a personal connection with the opposition, you slowly begin to lower their wall of protection for them to *begin* to listen to what My Great Aunt EDNA is saying. My Great Aunt EDNA just reminded me to tell you not to expect them to open up to you first. You must first make yourself vulnerable and share **personal** details. We're not referring to your kids and what they did the previous week (they don't care). We're referring to details of your failures, concerns, worries, and doubts you also possess. We're referring to what makes you weird, what insecurities you possess and so on. Like I said, these weapons are not for the faint of heart. As you earnestly share your inner being, they will begin to share theirs. At the point of connectivity, which will vary from relationship to relationship, you will have an "in" to begin to TELL, SHOW, and CELEBRATE Excellence.

Excellence – Confidence = Mediocrity

By show of hands (virtually), which one of you astute readers loved algebra in school? Which one of you cheated off the homework completed by the pretty girl/boy sitting to your right? (The one in front of you was prettier, but you couldn't see his/her paper). Which one of you loved algebra so much that you completed all your homework before you even left the class for the day? These are the people that will love this analogy My Great Aunt EDNA will use to illustrate the counterbalance of Excellence and Mediocrity, and the most important variable of Confidence.

As stated previously, the counter-spirit of Excellence is Mediocrity. However, one can be excellent and still have mediocre results. How is this possible? It is because one lacks confidence. A leader that lacks confidence, even though they have studied and practiced being excellent in their craft, is the equivalent of a meticulously designed and crafted gold watch that provides an inaccurate depiction of the time. It looks good, but it has lost its value and importance in respect to its purpose.

One of the best and worst movies of the 1980's is *The Last Dragon*, starring Taimak (Leroy Green), Vanity (Laura Charles), and Julius Carry (Sho'nuff). I LOVED this movie, and I have probably watched it fifty times. (In full disclosure, forty-nine of those times was because of Vanity. Damn, she was fine.) Very similar to other events that have occurred in my lifetime, this movie full of bad acting and cheesy graphics taught me a leadership lesson in my youth. Leroy Green, or Bruce Leroy as he was called in the movie, was desiring to become a *Master* in the Kung-Fu martial arts discipline. It was all he did, and all he loved. The last "Dragon," or master of Kung-Fu, was identified as Bruce Lee, and Leroy was mimicking him and seeking out knowledge from other elders to learn what was missing from his repertoire to become the Last Dragon. He worked tirelessly to perfect the art of Kung-Fu and was visibly better than anyone he went up against. Until he met Sho'nuff, the regional Kung-Fu bully. Every time Leroy had to fight Sho'nuff, the excellence he possessed was not enough to defeat his foe. It was not until Sho'nuff was holding his head under water and death was imminent for Leroy, and Sho'nuff yelling, "Who is the Master?!" that Leroy got the point. **He** was the Master, and he had acquired the excellence needed far above anyone else but had not accepted the confidence in his excellence to proclaim and believe his status. He lifted his head in triumph and added Confidence to his leadership equation and responded, "I am!"

So, if *Excellence − Confidence = Mediocrity*, let's do some algebra. Using the equation at the beginning of this paragraph, let us add Confidence to both sides of the equation. The new equation will then read, *Excellence = Mediocrity + Confidence*. The equation still balances out and creates a new truth utilizing the same variables. This new format of the equation is stating someone who is mediocre can add Confidence to their equation and arrive at Excellence. How many of you can remember a leader you had that was mediocre in their knowledge of their industry or organization, yet possessed exuberant confidence, which was noticeable to their team and arrived at excellent results? I know of many, and I have been in this situation before. I was recruited into banking as a Branch Manager with no banking experience. My team was obviously more knowledgeable than I pertaining to banking principles, yet the confidence displayed in leadership rallied my team to perform at a very high level. The Excellence in banking knowledge arrived later. Excellence in leadership does not require perfection. The most important variable is leadership confidence.

My Great Aunt Edna is very much like my grandmother, Bertha Mae Young. My grandmother had nine children whom she raised alone due to my grandfather's early death. Being the twin of my real great-aunt Edna, they both taught many of the same lessons without any formal education or work knowledge to support their teachings. However, all children and grandchildren can vouch for the Confidence displayed in the words and life-lessons from "Big Momma," and my great-aunt Edna. It is where the confidence in the leadership teachings shared from My Great Aunt EDNA derive from; two Black women born in Mississippi in the 1930's at the beginning of the Jim Crow era, who exuded Confidence, demanded Excellence, and preached against mediocrity.

Leadership is not a complex concept. Yet, many fail at it. There are leaders who have great confidence, yet they do not possess a spirit of Excellence that they enforce on their teams, therefore producing mediocre results. There are leaders that have a spirit of Excellence on their teams, but do not display Confidence, which causes doubt in the teams' direction, thus producing mediocre results.   And then, there are leaders that are just mediocre in general, including how they approach their own lives. None of these leadership scenarios will produce the results reached by nieces and nephews of My Great Aunt EDNA, who may have cheated off the paper of the girl/boy to their right, but learned and understood the algebraic equation necessary to pass the test of leadership.

Look for the Cracks

Excellence is sometimes birthed out of abstruseness. I love the representation of the mythical animal known as The Phoenix. Reborn out of her own ashes, the Phoenix is said to have recreated herself in a new and more powerful image, admired and feared by her previous adversaries. In leadership, many leaders are asked to take on situations that have been deemed convoluted and dire in terms of culture, business acumen, resourcing, or risk management. Weak leaders (definitely not in the family of My Great Aunt EDNA) will shy away from these challenges, because of the potential negative residue that can be attached to a leader's reputation and pride if they fail to make improvements. Nieces and Nephews of My Great Aunt EDNA will embrace these types of leadership opportunities because they understand the greatest stories are told and believed when an insurmountable challenge has been conquered, turning previous skeptics into ambassadors.

As a leader, one of the sweetest and savored sounds is the skeptic stating, "I did not believe that it was possible to turn this situation around, and I doubted that you were the right leader to do it. I must admit that you surprised me, and I have learned from watching your engagement with your team and peers." So how does a leader walk into a known situation of complexity, that requires circuitousness, and come out gleaming on the other side? They listened to My Great Aunt EDNA when she stated, "Look for the cracks."

To define a crack seems a bit infantile initially, but humor me for a moment. Close your eyes for 10 seconds, and then barely open one eye. What do you see? My assumption is you saw a glimmer of light. What you probably did not notice is that all of your attention immediately focuses on the crack of light, and not the surrounding darkness. You will start to wonder, what am I looking at? What image is on the other side of this small crack? Now obviously, you possess the power to completely open your eyes and see the image. Why? Because your brain has told you that you have the ability to do so, and so you do it. The same exists within leadership. A leader who believes they have the power to see the rest of the image and let in all the light that is available within that environment will do it. Just as with your eye, the light is let in incrementally, as you begin to take action.

So, what is the crack in your team environment? It will vary from team to team, and from experience to experience. Cracks can be one employee who thinks more positively than the rest of the team. A crack can be one new technology that makes processes more seamless or reduces risk. A crack can be a new training that grows the empirical knowledge and abilities of your team members. A crack can even be your own attitude change as a leader, and how you respond and listen to your teams' needs.

Now, let us think about the crack expansion in the inverse of letting in light. Think of the crack expansion in terms of removing darkness. In the universe created by God, the removal of darkness immediately invites in light. That is a good thing and practical for multiple reasons. In team environments, darkness can be represented in attitudes, language, outdated systems, human pride and envy, and the lack of the spiritual presence of Excellence. What darkness on your team needs to be removed to allow the crack to expand?

My Great Aunt EDNA has stated that Excellence is a spirit, and it is the initial presence that is required to create a leadership environment to fix shit and not break it again. Light and Excellence work together to bring forth the birth of new beauty from ashes. The trick is to look for the cracks, and then to not be distracted by the surrounding darkness.

Playing the Wrong Chord Can Make Beautiful Music with the Right Leader

Jazz music, in my opinion, is the most beautifully amalgamated concoction of music, science, art, intellect, imagination, and complexion of instruments that exists on the planet. Various forms of the genre express the dynamic and endless arrays of tastes that the music can deliver to one's melodic palate. I am bold enough in my love for the art to say I do believe Kenny G, is a jazz artist (Let's argue offline)! However, my favorite jazz artist of all time is Miles Davis. He is unequivocally the master of jazz, in my humble opinion, and the one artist who seems to be somehow connected to spiritual forces beyond the earth who gave him musical insight into the emotions of worlds we cannot see nor fully feel yet. His brain should have been studied after his earthly departure because it is not possible for a normal human brain to do what his did on that trumpet. **"So What?"** is my favorite, and **"Bitches Brew"** is mesmerizing.

Herbie Hancock is no one to sleep on either as a jazz artist. Herbie Hancock is one of the most renowned pianist/keyboard artists in the world and has composed some of the best-selling jazz records of all time. Herbie tells the story of being asked to play with the Miles Davis Quintet in 1963 and how excited and nervous he was to play with the jazz master. During one of the live performances early in their tenure together, Herbie was in his groove until something happened he would never forget. He played the wrong chord! It was a noticeable, blundering, and lingering wrong chord. So much so, Miles Davis stopped playing immediately in the middle of the live performance and looked over at Herbie for about two seconds. What happened next is what my Great Aunt EDNA would call leadership operating in the spirit of Excellence. Miles Davis then looked at the ground for about another seven seconds. The silence was awkward for both the band and the audience, until Miles did the work of a genius. He began to play notes that made Herbie Hancock's wrong chord right, while the band joined in. Amazing leadership!

As leaders, we must know our teammates will inevitably and eventually make some mistakes. Although we subconsciously know this will occur, as when Miles was in the middle of his live performance, we are normally not ready for them. What we do in the moment matters. It matters a lot, and it could steer the direction of your team member to become a deflated human with talent that is never materialized, or the next Herbie Hancock, composing and producing forty-one studio albums (forty coming after his live mistake), winning fourteen Grammy awards, and one Academy Award in 1986 for his original scoring of **Round Midnight.** As leaders, we can *choose* to operate in anger, disgust, disappointment, and embarrassment, or we can *choose* to seek to understand the mistake that was made and adjust our own actions to make the mistake a benefit for everyone involved.

One of the most fulfilling and emotional moments as a leader is when you watch a present or former team member receive their due recognition, knowing you have helped them learn from their mistakes in the past, which have equipped them with the necessary tools to reach their new point of distinction. I have had the great pleasure of seeing this moment materialize multiple times. But to be totally honest with all of you nieces and nephews of My Great Aunt EDNA, I have also had moments that I would like to have back as a leader. There were moments I was not prepared mentally or spiritually as a leader to be ready for the impactful mistake that was to come. I reacted poorly. I placed blame. I called them out. I attempted to distance myself from the mistake. I covered my own ass. My Great Aunt EDNA would have been disappointed in me. I was disappointed in me.

So how does one avoid having these moments as a leader when a teammate makes a mistake? I would suggest doing what Miles Davis did. I am not speaking of making the mistake a positive outcome, although that is the desired end goal. I am speaking of the preparation that occurred before the mistake. First of all, Miles already had to be in the right spirit as a leader to react the way he did. This takes personal time to develop your own personal emotions and well-being. He was definitely there. But here is the mesmerizing action that boggles my mind. Miles Davis was so good at his craft it only took him seven seconds to process the mistake, visualize the wrong notes in his mind, compose an entirely new adaptation to his song, and play in a way in which his band could pick up with him very quickly. He only wasted two seconds on the mistake. The rest of the time was spent figuring out how to make it right. Amazing leadership in the spirit of Excellence is what he displayed.

<u>Ok, let us argue for a bit. Kenny G, plays a more melodic R&B version of jazz, more structured in composition compared to the jazz greats, but he still lives within the emotional expression that jazz requires. Hit me up to debate. I'm ready!</u>

29 Drops, 41 Tackles

I begin this section by saying that the Arizona Cardinals suck this year. I can say that, because I am, and have been, a die-hard Arizona Cardinals' fan for many years. The rest of you non-Arizona Cardinal fans are only permitted to smile at my first statement for 5 seconds (and I will be counting), and then re-shift your focus back to the My Great Aunt EDNA leadership philosophy lesson that will eventually reveal itself in the forthcoming paragraphs.

The idea for this feature came to me from a consistent reader of the My Great Aunt EDNA content, who happens to be a young and emerging leader that I truly respect. Chris Caines is the Vice President of Economic & Social Justice for the Community Reinvestment Fund, USA. He is an astute and remarkably quirky, intelligent, and eclectic thought leader who also happens to be a sports junky. I love the mix of his personality that reflectively comes out in his leadership style, and you cannot help but like the guy.

Chris and I were recently discussing the spirit of Excellence, and he shared a remarkable statistic in the career of Larry Fitzgerald. Larry Fitzgerald is a retired wide receiver for the Arizona Cardinals who lives, breathes, walks, and talks the principles of My Great Aunt EDNA in Excellence, Doing Things the Right Way, No Shortcuts, & Accountability. He is a Hall of Famer for sure, and a respected leader in his field. Ironically, I sat about twenty feet from Larry recently at a Timberwolves vs. Suns NBA game. Chris Caines shared the statistic that Larry Fitzgerald only had 29 dropped passes his entire career! That is not a typo. In a 17-year career, with 1,432 catches, he only dropped the ball 29 times when it was thrown to him; mind-boggling! This is the epitome of Excellence in your craft, but this is not the reason I am writing about Larry.

For those of you not too familiar with American Football, the wide-receiver position is an offensive position. The statistic I am about to reveal is the reason why you aspiring and emerging leaders should pay attention. Larry Fitzgerald also had 41 tackles in his career. He had more tackles in his career, which is a defensive task, than he did mistakes in his offensive job role! So, why would Larry need to make a tackle you ask? Someone on his team made a mistake, and as a leader he immediately switched his job role to minimize the overall mistake impact to the team's ability to succeed. This is an amazing mindset that many leaders never develop. As a leader of leaders, one of my biggest pet peeves is when one of the leaders who reports to me begins a conversation with, "It wasn't me," and then puts forth no effort to mitigate the risks to the overall team.

My Great Aunt EDNA teaches that Excellence is a spirit. Here is a thought...is a spirit born, or made? Can a lazy, self-indulgent, yet talented wide receiver ever become a Larry Fitzgerald type of leader? In a business sense, can a narcissistic, career-ladder climbing leader, who plays the part of underwear (covering your own ass), ever immediately switch focus when a mistake is made by another teammate and go into Mission Possible-mode to mitigate risk? My Great Aunt EDNA says, yes. It is possible to "make a spirit." It is possible to make an intrinsic decision to cast off the spirit of selfishness and replace it with the garment of Excellence.

The first prerequisite to accomplish this is the admission of your current state of mental operation. If your mind has not been conditioned to think of the team first as a leader, it will be impossible for your unconscious self to immediately make the necessary adjustments. The types of tools necessary to "construct the spirit of Excellence" include meditation, reading, study, reflection, journaling, questioning, action, and lastly and most importantly, faith. Faith in the ability to accomplish this paradigm shift is necessary, and in my own personal case, faith in the willingness of God to guide me, as I will undoubtedly screw up on my own.

I am very thankful that Chris Caines reminded me of Larry's statistics. The statistics alone are staggering and immeasurable in comparison with any other performer in Larry's former world of playing football, but the leadership lessons are also just as staggering. This also reminds me there are other nieces and nephews of My Great Aunt EDNA who are learning and growing in leadership simply by observing and paying attention. Keep paying attention, Chris. God's lessons are everywhere.

BFF, Dudes, Homegirls, and Potnas

I have a few golden gems for you to use in your next team settings. *Why did the little boy run around his bed?* <u>To catch up with his sleep!</u> 😂 *Why did the snake sleep on the chandelier?* <u>It was a light sleeper!</u> 🤣 Ok, two more. *Why did the rooster cross the road in Thunder Bay, Ontario Canada*? <u>To make me late for dinner!</u> 😂🤣😁 I'm killing these jokes! Last one. *Why did the friendship come to an end?* **<u>One friend became the leader of the other!</u>** 😂🥴 That one is my favorite!!!

I often hear of friends wanting to go into business with each other, or one friend encouraging another to post for a job requisition where they will now be the leader of the same team they both are currently on. The initial thought is since they know each other so well, they will be a good balance in the team dynamic to offset each other's weaknesses (I'm smiling again). My Great Aunt EDNA gave me words of wisdom when I was a young leader. She said, "Baby, you can be *friendly* with your team when you are their leader, but you can't be their *friend*." As usual, My Great Aunt EDNA was right.

Let us distinguish between the differences of friendly and friend. I, like many of you I assume, have very few friends. These are people who I take vacations with, know the intimate details pertaining to their marriages, adulteries, kids, health, finances, criminal records (I have a few of those friends), dreams and aspirations, and the "crazy" of their families. They know the same about me. They are true friendships that last throughout many seasons of life. However, I have been friendly with thousands of people! Being friendly may include, happy hours (several), hugs, sharing pet pictures, sporting events, business travel, laughs, gifts, and solid memories.

So why is it important **_not_** to be a direct leader of your friends? It is because you are *intimate* with your friends, and words and actions directed to a friend will be perceived differently and hurt longer than the same words spoken to someone on your team you are simply friendly with. Excellence requires honesty and coaching, and honesty spoken to a friend in a leadership situation can be misconstrued as elitism or you just being an asshole. Unfortunately, the relationship that took so many years to build can be torn apart in a few short "leadership" phrases that were intended to be a positive impact for the team.

My Great Aunt EDNA always recommends that one friend transitions to another team whenever a new situation will require one friend to be the leader of the other. And never, ever, ever, no never, go into business as a partner with a true friend. I made that mistake once, and it strained our relationship for a while. Luckily, we have since mended those wounds and have returned to our friendship foolery. Time was lost that cannot be recouped, and the business did not survive. I use my own personal experience as one example, but I know of dozens of similar stories.

Sick & Tired of Being Sick & Tired

Breaking point. Ready to quit. I can't do this anymore. This is not working. I do not see any way a positive outcome can come from this. Why am I here? No one listens to me anyway. I should never have said yes. I put my soul into this, and for what? I wasted years of my life on this. Shit, I am just sick and tired of being sick and tired.

That last sentence is what my Great Aunt Edna and her twin used to say all the time. It is the point one reaches when they have exhausted all their inner strength to go on, or so they think, before finally grasping for that last bit of air. It is that point you feel when you have given up on a situation, thinking through what you felt you have contributed to making it work (with a bit of self-pity I might add), and waving the white flag of surrender.

If you have been in leadership for any real length of time, you have experienced this and probably have mumbled many, if not all, of the phrases in the first paragraph of this section. I know I have. Leadership is not for the weak-hearted. It is not for the glory seekers. It is not for the self-elevating hypocrites. Leadership as defined by My Great Aunt EDNA is for nieces and nephews who will work their asses off to seek Excellence in spirit for the greater good of their team. With that said, what should a leader do who has reached the point of being sick and tired of being sick and tired, and Excellence seems an impossibility?

My Great Aunt EDNA suggests wholesale change is necessary whenever a leader has reached this point. There are many situations that can be considered a wholesale change, but I would like to cover a few that may change the direction of your team if you find yourself in this situation. The first and most obvious wholesale change is leadership change. However, this is not easy because it requires leadership humility and reflection. Not all leaders are willing to admit that a new leader may be able to accomplish what they have not been able to do. The most self-aware leaders, and the ones that truly have the team's best interest at heart, will voluntarily step down from their roles to allow a fresh leadership perspective to take root on a team. These are the leaders that I, and My Great Aunt EDNA, admire most. A lesson I will never forget was given to me by My Great Aunt EDNA: all leaders have a right place, a right purpose, and a right time. When any of the variables reach their expiration date, it is time to move on. This does not necessarily mean a leader was ineffective. It simply means there is a new place, purpose, and time waiting for that leader, where they can recreate a new environment of Excellence.

The second wholesale change possibility is the recreation of the team construct. This is a fancy way of saying you may need to get rid of your team members and replace them with new members who have a fresh perspective, which does not include cynicism. A team full of cynics will never achieve a spirit of Excellence. Whenever I have been asked to take on a new team that has been struggling, I automatically expect a certain percentage of that team to be replaced, either voluntarily or involuntarily. I never hit the panic button in the first couple of years as the team transitions to one that has a sense of purpose and a spirit of Excellence, and the faces of the team members evolve.

Changing the dynamics of a team is a tricky situation, as new members must have chemistry with the existing team. They must bring in new ideas, but without posturing in an attempt to elevate their own presence over the presence of the team. Understand that just as leaders have an expiration on their place, purpose, and time, so do the team members you bring in. Their own guiding spirit will allow them to add value to your team for a period of time, but they must also move on to become the most effective version of themselves at some point.

The last option pertaining to wholesale change necessary in situations of being sick and tired of being sick and tired is the most difficult one. The first two options were fairly straightforward: either I leave, or you leave (sounds like a marriage). This last option requires heart, intellect, humility, listening, and grit. Instead of a leader leaving, or constructing a new team, there is an option of purposeful redirection of the entire team's purpose, mission, and resourcing. This is the one I witnessed from my Great Aunt Edna and my grandmother Bertha, which I have taken with me in my leadership approach. This option requires direct speech, honest assessment, the willingness to let go of the past, and the recreation of a new vision, which does not have any traces of the old.

This sounds like an impossibility for any team that has been struggling with performing with a spirit of Excellence, but it is not. Maintaining the same team construct yet starting over to pursue Excellence must begin with the leader having a strong purpose to change, humility to admit misdirection, and a new passion. If these characteristics are not visibly noticeable to the team members, the wholesale change will not occur. The excuse of being an introverted leader in this instance will not work. A leader must overtly drive the wholesale change and allow the team to get behind their passion. Through osmosis, the team will eventually understand that although their leader still physically looks the same, a new leader stands before them with a new vision of Excellence. However, just as in the other examples, not everyone on the team will go along for the ride, and some will choose another direction. As a leader who is trying this approach, know this will happen and do not get distracted by the evolution of the team.

For those of you who are currently in the sick and tired of being sick and tired phase of your leadership journey, take the time to do an honest assessment of yourself, your team, and your purpose. There are more options to resolve this phenomenon than I have listed in this section, but something must be done. To stay in this phase is a disservice to yourself, your team, and the organization. My Great Aunt EDNA would ask that action be taken to move towards a spirit of Excellence in your life, your team's existence, and the organization's purpose.

Being Thankful for the Wilderness

The wilderness can be a calming place for many. Many people synonymously think of the wilderness with quiet, beauty, nature, and peace. Picture the calming streams, the smell of pine and flowers, the colors of green, blue, amber, and brown congregating to form picturesque scenes. Imagine lying on a hammock staring up at a sky full of stars next to a booming full moon that causes one to wonder and question life. Ah, the serene gift of God that is called the wilderness. But wait; what is that smell? Sniff, sniff. It smells like death wrapped in spoiled bacon. Is that a...? Awww damn, it is; a wild boar! Welcome to the wilderness.

Leaders enter into the wilderness too. It typically happens in a slow methodical manner, instead of a sudden and noticeable act. One day, you are busy with people to meet, questions to answer, reports to decipher, importance to feel, and decisions to make. Then, there is that one Thursday afternoon where you find yourself staring out of the window wondering what to do next. You question your importance to the organization and wonder if you have any creativity left inside of you. Then, you notice the one Thursday has turned into every Thursday and every other Tuesday where you are doing this. Then it happens; the Monday you show up to work with no excitement or passion for leading people at all. They can lead their own damn selves for all that you care. Welcome to the leadership wilderness.

Leadership is lonely. People who have never led other people do not understand this phenomenon. Considering the fact most leaders are always surrounded by the teams they lead, most people would assume leaders are never lonely. Ask any leader who has led teams, large or small, and they will tell you they have often felt alone during leadership tenures. So, why does this happen? My Great Aunt EDNA would suggest this phenomenon is due to the cognitive dissonance most leaders experience while leading others. Cognitive dissonance is defined as mental stress or discomfort experienced by an individual who holds two or more contradictory beliefs, ideas or values at the same time (Wiki). So, what are the two competing beliefs most leaders experience? The first belief is, "I am the right person to lead this team to Excellence." The second belief is, "I am not qualified, nor the right person to lead this team to Excellence." Regardless of how confident a leader is, or the accumulated previous successes they have had in leadership, I promise you this competing thought will enter the leader's brain. What happens next? Leadership wilderness.

During leadership wilderness, leaders will experience a few phenomena. The first is the feeling of self-doubt. The second is loneliness. The third is reflection and redirection. And the final phenomenon is the return to the fold with renewed boldness. I personally believe all leaders need to experience and return to the wilderness periodically. A lonely place is the perfect place to concentrate on you. Leaders spend so much of their time thinking about others they can inadvertently neglect their own self-care and needed adjustments. Lonely places force one to have an internal focus and to reconnect with their source of quiet, beauty, nature, and peace. For some, that source of "soular" energy is God. For others it is nature itself. Some leaders reconnect with a voice of reason in the form of an uncharacteristic mentor. Regardless of what that source of energy is, leaders in the wilderness will inevitably seek this out in order to reflect and redirect.

Since great leaders listen to My Great Aunt EDNA and understand Doing Things the Right Way is critical, the points of reflection usually include a review of how things have been done on the team, and how the leader may redirect this to change the direction of the team. But beware, there are wild boars in the wilderness. In a search to determine which things to do with your team, there will be voices and concepts that will be brought to your attention, which are not in your best interest. If something smells wrong, like death wrapped up in spoiled bacon, it likely is wrong. Do not make the mistake of running out of the wilderness in efforts to save your own leadership life, only to invite death to your team. One of these "wild boar" traps smells like ways in which a leader can profit and gain the limelight without any consideration as to how this may impact the team's performance. Another trap smells like built up anger expressed in sharp responses and withdrawn emotion. And the most infamous and deadly wilderness trap is falling in love with the word "I." If, during an attempt to exit the leadership wilderness, a leader displays any of these characteristics, the team will immediately notice and respond in kind.

I am overall thankful for every leadership wilderness moment that I have experienced in my career; and there have been many of them. Some wilderness moments last a couple of weeks, while others have lasted a couple of months. These moments of loneliness, reflection, redirection, and philosophical joyous returns to the team have formed the leader I am. The wilderness moments have forced me to seek counsel I would have otherwise forgone. These moments have forced me to look at my own behavior, swallow the reality of imperfection, and recreate a better nephew of My Great Aunt EDNA. They have taught me what the voices of the wild boar sound like, and the various forms in which the traps will present themselves. I have become a hunter of the wild boar now, and I smirk when the beast has the audacity to show its face to me. This is not to suggest that I will never again experience the wilderness of leadership, but I am now more equipped to maneuver the wilderness, while enjoying the beauty of solitude that loneliness provides.

<u>By the way, wild boar tastes great!</u>

Chapter 3: DOING THINGS THE RIGHT WAY

- Excellence
- Doing Things the Right Way
- No Shortcuts
- Accountability

Superglue Superheroes

Most people have the best intentions. I really believe that. There are those rare occasions when people intentionally act to be a disruption to your quest for leadership grandiosity, but I think it is fair to assume most people have the best intentions. Even Superglue Superheroes. They are those well-intentioned individuals who want to come to your rescue and tell you how things were done before you arrived as the new leader, and how you should stick to the proven methods of operation. In other words, these people are **stuck** in the past, and expect you to **stick** to their plan: Superglue Superheroes!

My Great Aunt EDNA speaks of Doing Things the Right Way, which is a critical component to leadership success. With My Great Aunt EDNA, No Shortcuts are allowed in her world, which breeds the necessity to do things the right way as established by the collective team. However, there is a broad difference between Doing Things the Right Way and doing the right things. Doing Things the Right Way is a constant. This principle never changes and is intransigent in an environment of Excellence. In contrast, doing the right things is an ever-evolving abstract, which adapts to an ever-changing business environment. This is where Superglue Superheroes may impede your progress to implement My Great Aunt EDNA into your teams. They are expecting you to utilize proven methods of operations that produced past successes, which may not be in the best interest of the business environment today. Their definition or understanding of what to do may conflict with what you as the leader deem as the right things to do in a given situation.

There is value in having Superglue Superheroes desire to come to your rescue. First of all, assuming most people have the best intentions, you can also assume they want to see you succeed as a leader. Potential for alliance is plausible, but you must first help them understand your position and philosophies as a leader. Secondly, they have historical insight that may include important details for you to consider when you are developing your own tactics for determining what things are right in the current team environment.

The best way to partner with Superglue Superheroes is to first allow them to speak, and actually listen to what is being stated. Repeating what you heard them say is a sure-fire way to help them understand that you are not dismissing their input. However, it is important very early in these discussions to establish that you are listening to their input and not taking direction as to what are the right things to do. If you wait to deliver that message, you may end up in a situation where there is an unstated understanding you are pursuing their old methods of operation. When you do decide to change direction, there is a good possibility they will receive that action as dismissal of their opinions and no longer consider themselves allies in your leadership success.

Superglue Superheroes can be an asset or a danger to your leadership results. The speed to recognizing them is important, and how you establish a partnership with them can influence the team's ability to move forward with establishing new tactics of operation. But beware; My Great Aunt EDNA says that once you do establish the right things to do, Doing Things the Right Way consistently is a key ingredient to performing at a high level of execution.

Coach George

Are you one of those crazy parents who try to encourage other people's kids to play sports? You know, the crazy kind that tries to dismiss the balancing act of practice, homework, travel to games, potential injuries, and the exorbitant fees?! You promise the cynical parents that by playing sports, children learn life lessons that will live with them for the rest of their lives, although they are currently only eight years old and are more concerned with cereal than life? You state playing sports teaches teamwork, sharing, fair competition, and how to navigate different personalities. You PROMISE them their child will enjoy it, and the percentage of children injured is extremely minute. I am that dude! 😊

I am that dude, because I was that kid. I have played multiple sports since the tender age of five, and I can remember more about my experiences in sports than I do the experiences with the 20+ girls I dated in middle school. The middle school girlfriend experiences taught me things as well; mostly about the psychological delicacies within relationships that would hauntingly amplify in years to come. But the sporting memories taught me life lessons, one of which I will share with you now.

My Great Aunt EDNA's leadership culture is about Doing Things the Right Way. One of my most vivid memories of this lesson presented itself when I was a fifteen-year-old football player in my Junior year for the Fulda Falcons in Fulda, Germany. My coach was the now memorialized Hall of Fame American High School Football Coach, Marcus George. Coach George is the winningest coach in the history of American High School football in Germany, and still someone I revere as a great leader of whom My Great Aunt EDNA would approve.

On this particularly sunny day during practice, Coach George had me playing running back for the practice squad, as we were focusing on our first-team defense that day. I was a starting wide-receiver, and second-string defensive cornerback, which meant that I was prime to play on the practice squad that day for the first-team defense to massacre.

Coach George called a "32 Dive" in the huddle, which means the running back takes the hand-off from the quarterback and then runs in the first gap on the right side of the center. For those of you who do not know football, this means a major collision is in your near future with a defensive tackle or linebacker. I should also mention I was only 5'6" and 135 pounds at the time. I skipped the 4th grade, which meant I was always younger and smaller than my peers. Play starts…I take the ball…collision occurs (thanks Dani Palmer)…I remember little…coach yells.

Since I was still coming to when the yelling started, I was under the impression Coach George was yelling at the defense as to how they reacted to the play. He was not. He was yelling at me. It sounded something like this. "Son, hit the damn hole! You're tiptoeing through the hole with no speed, and I know you run faster than that. I've seen it! Now get your ass back in the huddle and let's run the same play again!" I'm thinking, *"Did he just tell the defense the exact play we are running so they can ALL meet me in the hole?"* Great.

Play starts...I take the ball...full speed...helmet and shoulders low...run through the same hole...run through the defensive tackle's arm and keep my legs moving...collide with my friend Dani Palmer the linebacker...spin to the right off him...see daylight...run for another 10 yards before I'm brought down by my friend Shaun Lott. Coach George starts yelling again. This time it sounded something like this..."That's what I'm talking about son! It is not **where** you run the ball. It is about **how** you run the ball." The light bulb goes off in my dazed fifteen-year-old head. On the previous play, I did the appropriate mechanics as the play was designed. I started running when the play started...I lifted my left arm to take the hand-off...I ran to the appropriate hole. Technically, I did the right things. But I was not Doing Things the Right Way, as My Great Aunt EDNA would say.

Years after that play, I would contemplate the contrasting difference between the two identical plays, which occurred less than one minute apart. What Coach George was teaching me was you can do the same exact thing twice, with different results if you *begin* with the commitment of Doing Things the Right Way. Even with the entire defense knowing what I was getting ready to do, I was able to make significantly more progress than the previous half-assed attempt.

Kid vs Adult

As a mentor/coach/administrator, Coach George often dealt with kids in a disciplinary manner. Helping kids learn how to make good decisions is the final destination. But he would ask, "How can we help them process options?" Decision-making skills are often flawed. "How can we plant a seed that will grow into the mighty oak of decision making?" Kids, in trouble, came in to see him in many emotional states....defiant and sullen...subdued in fear of consequences ...confused and embarrassed. In every case, his first response was silence. Allowing them to settle and ponder their situation usually helped.

After a time, his second job was to get them to become introspective. His first question to them was, "Who am I about to speak to….your child or your adult?" Before he let them speak, he told them everyone has a wise, knowing adult and a child inside them. No matter how old you are, the child remains inside of you. It is easy to find grownups who let their inner child run their lives. You can find them every day. Think of the loud, rude, crude and often criminal behavior you see every day in your life. These are people who are led by the child inside. If you seek those who are led by their adult, look to the boardrooms, the pulpit, in powerful leadership roles….great moms and dads. Without the adult, everything would be in disarray. The world would be in turmoil. Many of those inner child-led people often face a discipline hearing of their own; the courts, the point of a gun/knife, prison, ridicule, or lack of opportunity for success. Those are all much worse than sitting in front of Coach George.

His job, in that short time span, was to help them learn to reach out to and consult their adult inside. How to reach the adult? Coach would say first, stop the immediate childlike response to the issue. Take a deep, deep breath and blow it out slowly…repeat…repeat….Second, count to ten. Third, ask yourself three questions: 1. Is this the right thing to do? 2. Will this action bring respect to me and my family? 3. Would a hero do this?

After he took them through this activity, he explained all he did is find the adult. This adult inside can be associated with our religion and good strong values taught by our parents/teachers/mentors. As he would tell them, "My child is alive and well, but my adult decides when to let the child out, and you can, too." Seed planted…

Coach Marcus George is such a good man and leader, he sent me the following note of inspiration after learning about his part in my book:

Mac, I think the greatest experience that we can have is failure. Most people avoid it like the plague. The greatest accomplishments are born of failure and most people miss failure out of fear of losing face. I have always had a child inside me that pushed me to my limits. Remember 1st grade and all the hands that went up when the teacher asked a question? Somebody laughs and we stop raising our hands. I have always marched with my inner child. I never stopped raising my hand. Needless to say, I looked out of place many times. I saw the gems that many did not see because I never thought we would fail. If we stumbled, we just got up and continued our journey with our eyes on the mountain top. I saw what you could be, not the stumble, the mistake, the failure. Those were simply another step in the journey. We only fail when we stop....Never stop.... Do it again until you win. – Marcus George

And to This Plan, I Thee Wed

Picture the scene. "I vow to be by your side for as long as life is in me. I promise to travel beside you during all of life's ups and downs. I will forsake all others, and I will always choose you a billion times over, not because I have to, but because I want to. And to this plan, I thee wed." Now imagine a leader has spoken these words in the witness of their team. It may seem far-fetched to imagine a leader saying these words publicly, but I can promise you this is how your teams hear it when a vow to follow a particular plan is made.

Making vows in general can be a very paralyzing event for humans. Vows require a promise to abide by the words spoken with the observation of witnesses, without having the ability to foresee the future and events that may impact or challenge the vow. The very concept of leadership has unspoken vows readily designed into the philosophical thought that an identified group of followers will place their trust and futures in the hands of someone else. Again, a scary thought if you take the time to think about it, but what happens when an audible vow made by a leader, in particular a vow that involves a plan, is made with witnesses? Is the leader constrained by his/her own words? Some leaders believe so, and some will follow their vow of plan execution literally to the grave.

My Great Aunt EDNA emphatically teaches that Doing Things the Right Way is an integral construct in the tool chest of creating a great leadership culture. Where My Great Aunt EDNA notices self-imposed challenges with some leaders is that in attempting to do things the right way, some leaders will promote a "right way" within a larger tactical plan, and vow to follow that plan. When the plan is mature in execution to the point of obvious path variation that was not intended nor advantageous, those same leaders can feel trapped by their "right way" advertising and never adapt the plan. The appearance of being a vow breaker, poor planner, or a leader bereft of stability and foresight can be, and unfortunately has been for some, the weight too heavy to permit plan adaptation.

The leadership lesson in this moment is to always allow for adaptation within a plan when establishing a plan of execution within your team, and truly differentiate between doing the right things and Doing Things the Right Way. Doing the right things should always be variable and understood by the full team, as well as adaptive as the landscape of the internal and external environments change. The second lesson, and one debatable on multiple levels, is making vows as a leader looks good on a video but can be the career-ending moment a leader will dread for the rest of their existence.

If vows are to be made by a leader to a team, the vows should be directly made in support of team and leadership development. Whenever a plan has to adapt, there is an innate opportunity to develop new leaders on the team. If no one is challenged by the need to change the plan, this means the new plan will not be adequate enough to accomplish the goal. The new challenges will create the opportunity to assign new role responsibilities to your team, which will inevitably grow your teams' experiences.

A leader who is married to a plan by a vow is a leader unprepared or unconscious of the variable impacts of existence. There is nothing wrong with plans in the essence of tactical execution, but never convince yourself or your team that only one plan is the right way to accomplish a goal.

Communication is the Key & the Lock

Why did God not make humans mute? You have to admit, we say some really stupid things. If we were only able to think stupid things, and not say stupid things, I am under the impression our functioning world would be a much better place. Am I alone in this assumption? Think about it, if the dumbest expression you've ever heard was never heard, wouldn't you be better off for it? Over the years, I have heard some really dumb expressions, both directly and indirectly. One of the reasons why Tik Tok is so famous is because people spend hours upon hours listening to and watching the dumbest communicators, which the world has to offer. It's literally a comedic break to see that people are really dumber than you are, after you know you have recently said some really stupid things, and then you can get back to your life feeling better about yourself.

Now with all of that being said, what about the fact that some really good and important communication, which should be stated, never occurs? Is that not just as impactful as the stupid expression that was stated? I argue this is even more important. If Mother Teresa only served the downtrodden of Kolkata, India, but never communicated the importance of her mission in relation to the Christian religion, would we even know who she was or contributed millions of dollars from around the world to her cause? If your spouse/partner never communicates their real inner feelings during your relationship, is it really a surprise you may find yourself a single individual in the near future? Bringing this back to My Great Aunt EDNA, in leadership, if you do not communicate honestly and frequently with your team, is it no wonder your team finds themselves a new work home?

In life, communication is the key and the lock. It is the key to healthy relationships, strong functional teams, diplomacy, intellectual growth, and organizational vision implementation. Conversely, it is also the lock to successful solution diligence, emotional collectiveness, shared vision, and may I add, intimacy. The lack of communication can be just as detrimental to teams as expressing a bunch of stupid things. Vocal cords have power beyond the audible sonic waves they create in the atmosphere. They have the power to penetrate mind, soul, and spirit. So much so the soul will begin to yearn for sound in the absence of its presence. However, the soul does not operate alone. The mind will covet something to interpret in the absence of communication and will eventually satisfy its pining with a substitute concept to ponder.

So, you are asking yourself at this moment, how does any of this relate to My Great Aunt EDNA or leadership? Doing Things the Right Way includes the absolute necessity for proper communication. How can one know what the right way is to do anything, if nothing has been communicated? Many leaders make the mistake of assuming their team members know what the right way to do something is, but they have never truly communicated this. It lives in their own brain and is likely very detailed and understood within themselves. Unfortunately God did not give us the ability to see beyond the calvarium, interpret its electronic pulses within the middle cranial fossa, and translate this into shit that makes sense to us. As humans, we require communication; vocal, signals, or otherwise.

Janelle Duray gave a great example of the importance of being properly communicated to in her early career, which helped her to know what the rights things to do were. Janelle is the Executive Vice President, and Chief Operating Officer for Jobs for America's Graduates (JAG). She began her tenure with the organization as an intern and shared how the 39 state affiliate leaders made clear to her what their needs were. As an enthusiastic young leader sometimes does, Janelle would jump right into attempting to solve their pain points, yet "do the wrong things." She stated the affiliate leaders would constantly guide her by further explaining the details of the needs. These repetitive communication corrections taught Janelle how to listen properly for pain points, as well as how to address similar ones with her external stakeholders. Janelle now works with 14 United States Governors, who serve on JAG's board of directors, as well as their staff, to create national programs that drive impact at the state level.

However, her real challenge, and the executed learned lessons of properly communicating appeared during 2020, when she was promoted into her current position as Executive Vice President during one of the most difficult crises the world has experienced, COVID-19. The majority of the work that JAG does is designed to be conducted inside the schools of the United States. Immediate communication needed to occur internally, and with external student engagement, to understand how to continue to engage students in a virtual environment. By maintaining this sound discipline of communication across various channels in new formats, she was able to help move JAG into its most ambitious three-year strategic plan in the history of the organization.

In leadership, communication needs to be frequent, multi-channeled, and most important, honest. I cannot begin to tell you how much I personally hate "corporate communication" from leaders, which is laced with padded words to appease, half-inform, deflect, and ultimately deceive the receivers of the communication. The sad thing is that corporate leaders who reach a certain level of leadership are actually taught how to do this with the assistance of script writers, lawyers, and professional bullshitters. It is a sad state of affairs, and no wonder employees begin to quietly quit after exposure to multiple episodes of this.

My Great Aunt EDNA is a firm believer in communicating honestly, so the team members are properly equipped with the necessary understanding to Do Things the Right Way. She also believes in not withholding communication that can assist the team in either gaining understanding or working to establish intimacy that leads to trust. People are much smarter than we give them credit for. As leaders, give them something to focus on, using proper and honest communication as the key. Do not allow communication to become your team's lock.

The Law of Diminishing Returns

I could never have predicted that when I was in school, I would be willingly writing about subjects I absolutely hated at the time. Economics was one of those subjects. I think I actually daydreamed about being the sixth member of New Edition (pre-Johnny Gill) through an entire class. I had written "our" next **#1** hit called "CONNIE," co-produced the jam with Babyface, choreographed the dance routine, and married Apollonia in one class period. That's what I call efficiency.

Apparently, I was not completely inundated with being an R&B sensation, because somehow the law of diminishing returns crept its way into my being, and I have never forgotten the theory. I can remember the moment when the theory shifted in my consciousness from economics to life. It was a eureka moment in slow motion, staring at the graph that my teacher had drawn, and realizing the impact this theory has on the outcomes of people's lives. Wisdom is a subtle and sneaky whisper, and if you pay attention to its voice, you can avoid pitfalls, get ahead faster in life, and reap the benefits of its direction. This was a wisdom moment for me.

The law of diminishing returns is a theory in economics, which predicts after some optimal level of capacity is reached, adding an additional factor of production will actually result in smaller increases in output. Fascinating, and true! In simple terms, this theory states if all other variables remain constant, and you keep adding the same thing that you have previously added to increase production in an area, eventually the outcome you are desiring to improve will start to diminish and could result in a negative margin if you do not change your approach. In summation, the third stage of this law specifically deals with overutilized inputs.

Let us examine this theory through the lens of leadership and the culture of My Great Aunt EDNA. Great leaders spend an enormous amount of time creating an environment that contains the appropriate variables and conditions to optimize outcomes. The really great leaders can identify the one variable condition that they can control, which will give their teams an immediate marginal increase in production. The leaders will naturally continue to press the big red button that activates this controlled variable, expecting similar results. But here lies the blind spot; without adjusting any other variables in the conditional equation, and by not measuring the marginal increase over time, leaders can be lulled into a situation in which their teams are no longer performing, and they do not understand why this has occurred. The answer: The law of diminishing returns.

My Great Aunt EDNA teaches that Doing Things the Right Way is a critical component to creating a leadership environment where the spirit of Excellence thrives. This is an accurate assessment of one of the variables to leadership success. However, she has never stated that a leader must always do the same things, the same way, in perpetuity to be successful. Via metamorphosis, evolution, and wisdom, a leader must be able to measure and distinguish when production additions of the "right way" have begun to diminish production outcome. The beauty of understanding the impact of the law of diminishing returns is you begin to understand there will ALWAYS be a point in time in ANY production environment (be it work, marriage, parenting, friendship, or making songs and videos with New Edition) at which a maximum point will be reached, leaving only a downward trend in the future production graph. As a leader, you must be cognizant, prepare for, and adjust variables and approaches to continue in a positive production environment.

I am purposely attempting to rile emotions and conversations with this next statement. Consider the United States of America, and how the production graph of this country exploded in ways the world has never seen over a short time period of only two hundred years. The United States led world production in almost every single measured category of economics, wealth accumulation, education, art, innovation, music, military, and science for a hundred years. This country is no longer #1, or even in the top 10 in most of the categories listed. Why? The law of diminishing returns. Our leaders have attempted to increase production without changing any of the controllable variables, because success had previously been achieved with a particular model. Sadly, some have even attempted to recreate the model and "Make America Great Again," assuming that the same production model will achieve the previous results. Blind spot. The future success of this country will require a change in the production model, along with the wisdom to measure and understand when a marginal increase will diminish production in the new format.

     I ended up receiving an A- in my Economics class. Once I realized I could apply a boring topic to me at the time, to life, I was far more interested in paying attention. I am by no means an economic genius, but I do know how to use those theories in my leadership and life scenarios. You can do the same. Leadership is simply a conglomerate of life experiences and mishaps, packaged up nicely to assist others in becoming their best selves.

<u>Lastly, "Connie" should have been a hit. She sat in front of me in class, but I never had the opportunity to sing the song for her.</u>
<u>Tragic.</u>

Betting on Myself

Betting on yourself. The first person that came to mind when writing this title was Pete Rose. For all of you non-baseball fans, or readers under the age of forty, Pete Rose is one of the best baseball players to ever play the game. He played for the Cincinnati Reds from 1963-1986, and he was a household name during my youth. However in 1989, he was banned from baseball after being found to have placed wagers on his own games. He is not in the baseball Hall of Fame, although many argue he should be. I have an opinion as well. Contact me, and we'll talk about it.

This title came directly from the mouth of one of the most influential leaders in recent times, in my opinion. His name is Kurt Grossheim, and he is the President and Chief Executive Officer of Global Holdings LLC. My introduction to Kurt occurred while he was the Chief Operating Officer for Synchrony, and I was the Vice President of Operations Optimization for the Consumer Bank. Kurt's extensive career spanned both domestic and international financial services, including roles in business leadership, banking, operations, client development, business development and integration, risk management, and regulatory affairs. Earlier in his career, Kurt worked for GE Capital and served in a wide range of leadership roles across multiple businesses and functional disciplines in the US and internationally. Some of his roles included President and CEO of GE Money Bank, SVP and General Manager for one of GE Capital's largest credit card portfolios, and CEO of GE Capital Bank in Austria.

During a recent discussion with Kurt, he and I recalled a statement he made on an all-employee call during the announcement of his transition from Synchrony. On this call with the entire Enterprise Operations team of 10,000+ team members, Kurt made the statement that he wanted to take a risk, and "Bet on myself." I will never forget his statement, because in my mind, and I am sure in the minds of others on the call, here was a leader who had "made it," "living the dream," "ballin' out," "been there and done that," and still desired to push himself. During our conversation, Kurt used the term "ambitious" to describe himself and hinted he may seek even greater impact in his career before it is all said and done. I could only smile inside and admire his spirit.

For true leaders, the job is never finished, because there will always be people who need to be influenced, encouraged, taught, directed, assisted, recognized, and promoted. I am sure there are those who may think Kurt's ambition, and utilizing the statement of "Betting on myself," signifies traces of narcissism. I beg to differ. My eyes, having been conditioned by the leadership culture of My Great Aunt EDNA, see a leader who has not poured out everything God has filled him up with prior to his birth; and Kurt recognizes this. I would even argue leaders who have "arrived" in their own minds when they achieve certain executive blah, blah, blah titles, and have a certain level of wealth, which they are afraid to place at risk, are the narcissists, withholding leadership nuggets that could be scattered about more broadly.

A true leader will think like Kurt and say, "How else can I make an impact?" "What other avenues and vehicles can I utilize to share this gift of leadership?" "Who else needs my assistance, and how can I get it to them?" "What mistakes have I made that I can share with others to help them avoid delays in their own career progression?" "What other leaders do I need to connect with and learn from, to continue to grow?" My guess is there is someone at Global Holdings LLC reading this and saying to themselves right at this very moment, "I am very glad Kurt decided to bet on himself and place his position of comfort at Synchrony at risk to come to our team." In Kurt's own words, "The easy decision would have been for me to stay at Synchrony. We were rocking and rolling with a great company. I had to ask myself, am I too much in a comfort zone?" Although I personally did not want to see Kurt leave Synchrony, I am also very appreciative of the example he set for me and others who are truly paying attention.

Kurt spends a great deal of time discussing Doing Things the Right Way. It is who he is. He explains how a culture of Excellence can only be achieved by everyone on the team Doing Things the Right Way, and not allowing mediocrity to become the norm. His passion for Doing Things the Right Way is birthed from his sentiment that the fear of failure is as motivating as the opportunity for success. This fear of failure as a leader causes him to always consider the next iteration and evolution. Anytime iteration is necessary, risk is inherent. There will be the risk that what came before the next iterative period will have reputational perception impact. There will be the risk the forthcoming metamorphosis will impact future opportunities. Lastly, there is the risk your damn bank account can be impacted. This is what keeps most narcissistic leaders from continuing to share their leadership gifts.

I applaud Herr Grossheim-type leaders, who will bet on themselves, take a risk, and dare to influence more people and organizations when they do not have to. I applaud nieces and nephews of My Great Aunt EDNA who focus on Doing Things the Right Way in order to achieve levels of Excellence, even when no one else is watching. I applaud leaders who place their own comfort at risk, place a bet, and know that even if they do not win exponentially, they have won the hearts and minds of their teams. The evidence of this is the fact I am writing this about Kurt when I do not have to.

Chapter 4: NO SHORTCUTS

- Excellence
- Doing Things the Right Way
- No Shortcuts
- Accountability

Baby Don't Rush

Do you have those one or two songs you play on repeat on a spring day with your windows rolled down? No one is in the car with you, and you just cruise, meditate, reminisce, and smile. The sun is shining, and your lean in the car is just a bit different. One of those songs for me is **"Don't Rush,"** by Kelly Clarkson, featuring Vince Gill. It is one of those chill Country songs with a 70's feel, sprinkled with a touch of R&B for good measure; just enough beat to make you slowly bob your head while you're listening to the message in the lyrics. The title gives it away, but the message is to slow down and enjoy the moment.

One line of that song reminds me of a message from My Great Aunt EDNA. Kelly says, "Throw the map out the window, taking the long way around." Such a profound lesson for couples, and by the way, leaders as well. One of the failed strategies I witness from leaders is the approach of following a business map established by a previous leadership regime, and then deciding to take shortcuts when they realize the map wasn't created for them. Mistake, mistake, mistake. The first mistake is utilizing a map created by a previous leader. The second mistake is taking shortcuts. The third mistake is taking shortcuts.

Let's discuss the first mistake of utilizing another leader's business map. I would like to illustrate this point by a lesson I learned from my 8th grade science teacher, Mr. Pereza, in Ft. Huachuca, AZ. Mr. Pereza taught me about the Amoeba. An amoeba is a unicellular organism that has the ability to alter its shape, primarily by extending and retracting pseudopods (Wikipedia). Mr. Pereza had us watch hundreds of amoeba cells through a microscope to notice how the amoebae swim in a pattern. It is as if you are watching a synchronized swimming routine of cells without hearing the music they are swimming to. Then, Mr. Pereza instructed us to drop one single drop of a foreign substance into the liquid and look again. Immediately, the amoebae speed up and swim around frantically! As all the 8th graders began to get loud and scream "Cool!" he shouted louder,

"Keep watching!" As we reengaged with the microscopes, what we noticed was the amoebae would begin to slow down, and then one *new* leader would begin to swim in a *new* pattern. The amoebae would all follow, and eventually a new swimming pattern was developed. Same team, new leader, new pattern. The same is true in business leadership. When a new leader is introduced into an already synchronized culture, chaos will ensue, and the team will not begin to follow the new leader until he/she swims in a different pattern than the previous leader. Throw the map out the window. It wasn't designed for you.

Now, for the second leadership mistake of taking shortcuts, my Great Aunt EDNA thought it important enough to include it in the meaning of her name. Simply put, no shortcuts allowed in good leadership. Why, you ask? Shortcuts inherently remove experiences that are necessary for the growth of your team. Is it possible to achieve the same results by taking shortcuts? Of course. As a reminder, the spirit of Excellence is illustrated in the *how*, not the what. To create a culture of Excellence, a leader must do as Kelly Clarkson instructed and take the long way around. Another metaphor illustrating the same thought is to take the scenic route. In your leadership plan, allow your team to *see* the good, the bad, and the ugly associated with achieving a desired result. Shortcuts will only short-change your team and limit your ability to create sustainable leaders who follow you. Baby, don't rush it. Just lean a little more in your car and play it back.

Which is Heavier, Money or People?

Let us imagine a zero-gravity condition. All things weigh the same in zero-gravity. Imagine thumping an elephant with the slightest of touch, and it travels the same distance, and moves with the same fluency and ease as when you thumped an ant seconds before. In this zero-gravity environment, you can lift a person as easily as you lift paper currency. Obviously, we either need to travel outside of the Earth's atmosphere, or to the nearest Zero-G experience fun-park to accomplish this physically. However, philosophically, we only need to travel inside our thoughts as leaders to lift money and people equally.

Several leaders reading this have come face-to-face with the challenging decision of lifting people or lifting money as their priority. They struggle with the weight of balancing an income statement and balance sheet, and simultaneously inspiring and lifting the people who follow them. Not always, but many cases I have personally witnessed are grounded in the root cause of a leader previously taking shortcuts on one or the other, and now being faced with how to recover what was lost due to the shortcut decisions.

My Great Aunt EDNA vehemently stresses that No Shortcuts should be taken in leading a team in the spirit of Excellence. The smoke and mirrors associated with taking shortcuts is that it temporarily appears you have accomplished something faster and possibly with more efficiency than if you had taken the appropriate route towards completion. The reality displayed when the smoke clears is you are left with a final product void of all the necessary components to equally lift money and people with the same required amount of leadership exertion.

Let us focus on the weight of money. Weight of an inanimate object in business can typically be measured in what the object is requesting from you. In business leadership positions, money asks you to sell something so you can acquire more of it, manage expenses so profitability can be made, invest it so residual income paths are created, and finally, it asks leaders to pay for the services utilized to acquire it. The inability, or lack of effectiveness to accomplish any of these asks can add to the weight money places on the shoulders of a business leader.

Now, let us look at the weight of the asks that people put on a leader. People ask for livable and fair wages in exchange for the services required to help the leader meet the demands money has requested, fair and equitable treatment and opportunities, confidence in the organization's ability to deliver on its promises it made to "money," and lastly, and most important to My Great Aunt EDNA, inspiration. People want to be inspired by their leaders, and this may be the heaviest weight of all.

Back to the original question: which is heavier, money or people? An argument can be made that money is heavier on the shoulders of a leader, because without meeting its demands, there is no business. A competing argument is that people are heavier. People have elements of a human soul that are variable in nature, which may constantly imbalance the weight they place on leaders. People are unpredictable, whereas money (to some leaders) is an inanimate object, which can more easily be controlled.

I'll let you in on a little secret. The point of this discussion is not about which one is heavier. The point of this discussion is to force you to think of ways to create a zero-gravity environment, so that neither weight is pressing upon the team. The truth is both money and people are extremely heavy weights for leaders to carry, and unfortunately, many leaders spend a large majority of their time focused on how they can reduce the weight of either, or both. Wrong focus. In every situation I have observed leaders focus on Excellence without taking shortcuts, I have also witnessed team environments that carried no weight. The critical factor is the environment, not the objects. A "zero-gravity" environment is one where people look forward to coming to work. They do not feel the "gravity" of leadership pressing upon them to produce. They willingly produce because they enjoy being there and being a part of something greater than themselves. In other words, they are inspired.

When people are inspired, they help the leader meet the demands money has asked of them, and truly desire to make it as weightless an effort for the leader as possible. This is the environment of "zero-gravity." This is the environment that nieces and nephews of My Great Aunt EDNA should aspire to create. Do not get lost in the objective weight of the asks upon you. Get lost in the weightless universe you create through inspiration.

Chapter 5: ACCOUNTABILITY

- Excellence
- Doing Things the Right Way
- No Shortcuts
- Accountability

Accountability is Caring

The thirteen-year-old me had mommy issues. I could have sworn I had the meanest mother on the planet earth. I mean, she was downright cruel. She made me do things like make my bed, clean my room, do homework, get good grades, take baths, be nice to my little sister, say sir and ma'am, and worst of all, wash dishes! I would have volunteered to eat with my hands for the rest of my life if I never had to wash another dish. I would have pulled a Chris Rock in the movie, "*I'm Gonna Git You Sucka*," and said, "F-it! Just poor the damn drink in my hand!" I even had to answer the house phone (back when those existed) with the phrase, "Thank you for calling the McNeil residence. This is Simon speaking, how may I help you?" I'm not joking. I had to say it just like that.

My friends would come over to my house and say, "Bro, your mom is mean." I would politely state, "Yep." If I wanted to go to the movies, she would inspect my room first, and then the den (which was one of my chores), and then answer with, "Ok, wash the dishes and you can go." George Lucas and Steven Spielberg both contributed to the cleanliness of my house. My best friend Dexter Johnson attributed the cleanliness of his apartment as an adult to my mother, because he would help me wash the dishes on multiple occasions as a teenager so we would not be late to the movies; true story.

All of this is to say my mother was, by no definition of the word, mean. She was teaching me about Accountability, which she learned from her mother, my great aunt Edna's twin. She was teaching me that once you are given responsibility, you are expected to accomplish the tasks assigned to the role with no exceptions; and she allowed, no exceptions. Had my mother allowed exceptions in her expectations of me, she would have in essence been teaching me she really did not care for me as a son or a person.

A great leader whom I personally respect recently spoke to me about this very concept in how he leads his teams. Ed Brinson is a General Manager of American Airlines, running their operations in Ft. Walton Beach-Destin, FL. This destination is one of the most sought-after vacation destinations in the country, so you can imagine how busy he and his teams are year-round. Ed has been in leadership for over twenty years, and he has extensive experience in leading people. He describes his business as "the people business," even though he is responsible for getting very large and complex engineered systems into the stratosphere to arrive safely at predestined locations.

During a recent interview Ed participated in for the My Great Aunt EDNA YouTube show, he stated "As a leader, if you are not holding your people accountable, you are part of the problem." This statement resounded in me, and I immediately began to ponder the ebb and flow of my own leadership career. To be completely honest and transparent, I have been part of the problem a few times as a leader by not fully holding my teams accountable. My Great Aunt EDNA is a firm believer in Accountability, and I do my best to adhere to her leadership philosophy. However, I have had moments in leadership where Accountability has taken a back seat to other matters.

Ed Brinson also expressed that Accountability is caring, which reminded me of my mother. He believes if a leader does not truly care for their team, they will simply let them fail and replace them with another team member. The lack of Accountability is the expression of a non-caring leader. Accountability, when partnered with coaching, can be the determining factor in a team member growing and reaching their full potential in their own career. When a team member is held accountable with consistency, what naturally begins to happen is the subconscious adaptation of self-accountability. The team member will eventually feel uncomfortable with foregoing expected tasks, and the unsettling feeling in their spirit will force them to readjust their behavior to the level of Excellence to which they have grown accustomed. A personal example of this is the difference between how I approached homework as a teenager, versus how I approached homework as a working adult completing college courses in the evening. I no longer needed my mother to hold me accountable. Her previous consistency had created an expectation within me that forced me to complete the work and find fulfillment in doing so. That is demonstrated care in actuality.

      Courtnie Coble is the Founder & CEO of The Academy of Goal Achievers. Her organization provides leadership and mentoring programs for high school students, and she is making a huge impact on the next generation of leaders who will emerge. Passion for her purpose exudes from her pores, and during a recent interview with me she expressed how her standards of Accountability not only help to prepare her students and their parents for the future expectations that will be placed upon them, but also how Accountability is a staple within her organization's culture, which helps to sustain the business. Courtnie explained that as she works to help place students in corporations and college opportunities, she is adamant with them that being accountable to their promises is not an option. She explains to the parents and students how a lack of accountability on their part can not only impact the student's future opportunities, but that it can also impact the reputation of The Academy of Goal Achievers and subsequently impact the opportunities of students who come behind them. Her care for the students and parents in her program is demonstrated in how Accountability is not presented as an option to remain in the program.

      I recently had a brief conversation with the leaders who report to me about the difference between the relationship of being a friend with your direct reports and being friendly with them. A few of them took exception to my point that I was not their friend, but that I am very friendly with all of them. I can understand why they would feel that way, as we have a lot of fun together, and I genuinely like each and every one of them. However, I care for them more than I desire to be their friend. Why? Because I need to hold them accountable to Excellence in order for them to be their best. I pray for them daily to succeed and grow beyond their roles on my team. That is the ultimate goal in me leading others, and My Great Aunt EDNA, Ed Brinson, and my mother would be disappointed in me if I showed a lack of care by not holding them accountable.

<u>*Now, go make your bed and wash the dishes!*</u>

I Did Not Ask for This

Leadership by default can be both unwelcome and a blessing at the same time. There is a long-standing debate that asks whether leaders are born or made? I tend to believe leaders are made. Some are made through mentorship and example, and others are simply made to do it. You know the stories; an employee who has no aspirations to lead others or take responsibility for a team, but since they are the most tenured employee when an unfortunate situation causes an untimely leadership opening, they are promoted. Or a failing location or department has terminated their previous leader, and a new leader is forced to take on the responsibility of the struggling team. This event is typically followed by moaning and bellowing, anxiety, Rolaids, sleepless nights, social media rants, and eventually the settling of nerves and acceptance of the new reality.

The environment of success within the team is irrelevant at this juncture. If the team is successful, the new leader may dread taking the blame for any decrease in performance. If the team is struggling in performance, the leader may dread having to find a new path of leadership for successful results. A typical first thought in this leadership situation is to ponder accountability. Should the leader deflect all success and failure to the previous regime, or should the leader accept full accountability for everything that occurs going forward?

My Great Aunt EDNA says all team members should be held accountable for the team's performance, but it always begins and ends with the leader. My Great Aunt EDNA suggests that after receiving responsibility, a leader should begin the first team meeting with the topic of Accountability. Definitively and clearly stating ownership accountability is a very expedient way to begin to win the confidence of a new team. **Everything** a new leader says <u>and does not say</u> will run through the mill of leadership accountability and team confidence until the team is fully confident in the new leader.

The cousin of accountability is realistic expectations. They grew up together. I cannot stress this enough; it is very important for a leader to establish realistic expectations in terms of time, resources, and performance measures with their team and their immediate supervisors. The worst-case scenarios begin with a leader establishing unrealistic expectations of performance to exacerbate their new leadership profile, followed by ownership in accountability to ensure that measures are met. The weakest of appointed leaders will respond with "I Did Not Ask for This," as a protective layer when the measures are not met. New leaders that are following My Great Aunt EDNA's leadership cultural advice will know to establish realistic expectations, even if it is not what their peers or leaders want to hear. Your team will appreciate you for this later.

The flip side of the initial heat of taking on a leadership position you did not ask for is, as Stuart Scott of ESPN's Sportscenter used to say, "As cool as the other side of the pillow." The potential outcome of what some may deem as fate is a new and successful leader. Some of the best things in life come from opportunities you personally did not ask for. I personally did not ask to move to California to become a District Manager for JPMorgan Chase. Leaders asked me. I personally did not ask to become an Operations Market Manager with Bank of America. Recruiters asked me. I personally did not ask to become VP of Optimization for Synchrony Bank. Synchrony asked me. So on, and so forth. The moral of the story is that leadership opportunities present themselves to nieces and nephews of My Great Aunt EDNA who are willing to accept accountability, set realistic expectations, and then move forward in the spirit of Excellence. "I did not ask for this," is an inappropriate and possibly self-deprecating response to being "made" to lead.

Four Uses for Your Leadership Thumbs

Your thumbs can be considered the "Swiss Army Knives" of your body. You utilize them a lot more than you consciously notice, and the absence of them will inevitably force other members of your body to do more work. I like to think my thumbs are incredibly sexy. No one on earth has ever told me this, but they are very well manicured, brute in appearance, yet soft to the touch (kind of creepy, I know). Without my thumbs, my life would be much different. I am not speaking of physical limitations. I am speaking of leadership limitations.

In keeping with the theme of Accountability that My Great Aunt EDNA speaks of regularly, the use of your leadership thumbs can make or break the perception of your leadership accountability. The four uses of your leadership thumbs as suggested by My Great Aunt EDNA are 1 – Pointing them at yourself , 2 – Hitchhiking, 3 – Creating space, 4 – Recognition.

Pointing them at yourself

When your thumbs are pointed at yourself, versus utilizing your pointing finger directed at others, a leader is accepting self-accountability. This characteristic is the very essence of leadership, which attracts long-term followers. Regardless of the situation, my Great Aunt EDNA expects her nieces and nephews to assess their own participation in successes and failures. Notice that I stated both successes and failures. Leaders should not only be permitted, but encouraged, to point their thumbs towards themselves in situations of success as well. While some see this type of gesture as braggadocious, it is only right that a leader accepts some level of responsibility for successes if the team expects a leader to accept responsibility for failures. My Great Aunt EDNA once told me, "Buy your own cake, make your own plaque, and plan your own party when team success occurs. Because people will most definitely expect you to plan your own funeral, buy your own flowers, and write your own eulogy when your team fails."

Janelle Duray provided another great example of the concept of pointing your leadership thumbs at yourself, which should be an encouragement and guide for any leader reading this book. She stated that as a younger leader, she struggled with the comprehension that anyone would want to take an interest in her or her accomplishments. In her mind at the time, she was just "little Janelle from the farm, a little intimidated, and simply appreciative that she even lived in the city of D.C." Now, she states, "I'm shameless." She encourages young women who may feel this way to lean into those opportunities, and set up conversations with other leaders with whom you are impressed. She proudly states, "You are special. You are worth it, and you deserve to have a seat at the table."

Hitchhiking

For those who are not familiar with hitchhiking, let me explain the concept. Back in the day, when humans were naïve, trusting, and had the soul of the Good Samaritan mentioned in Luke 10 of the Bible, all you had to do was stand on any street with traffic, put your thumb up vertically when a car drove by, signifying that you needed a ride somewhere (pre-Uber and Lyft), and someone would eventually stop and offer you a ride. In other words, you would utilize the vehicle of another to get from where you were currently to where you desired to go. Hitchhiking in leadership is one of the best ways to move you and your team quickly from one point to another.

Contrary to popular belief, leaders do not need to create the vehicle, search for the fuel to power the vehicle, and then know the route to get their team from Bland Street to Party Central Avenue. I have often hitchhiked on the vehicle created by other leaders to carry my teams to success. As an example, I once hitchhiked on the ideas created for leading a New Build banking district for which I was given responsibility. A good friend of mine and great leader, Brian Giles, was one of the first New Build District Managers for JPMorgan Chase in Southern California. He did a marvelous job of recruiting talent, designing New Build branches, establishing pre-opening marketing and sales strategies, and then launching successful branches. When I transitioned into the role of New Build District Manager and moved to California, I quickly admired and utilized Brian's strategies and tactics to open several successful branches myself. The concept was not mine; there was already a framework in place created by another leader, which I utilized to lead my team to success.

As in the original concept of hitchhiking, payment after the ride is not mandatory but appreciated. The ideological concept of hitchhiking involves the payment method of paying it forward. Help someone else when you have the ability to do so. Help another leader succeed. Allow them to utilize your vehicle. One of the greatest compliments I have experienced while leading others is when another leader utilizes My Great Aunt EDNA to create the leadership culture they need on their team to drive success.

Samantha Melting is Head of the Consumer Bank for Synchrony. She has vast responsibility that spans multiple continents, and she recently shared with me how one of her former bosses earlier in her career helped her to become the leader she is today. It is obvious when speaking with Samantha, that "Brian" had an influential fingerprint on who she was able to become. She stated, "He was the leader who believed in giving his team a voice, and a time in the spotlight. But he was also the one who would cut through the BS and just say, tell me what you want." She explained that in high profile meetings, he would purposefully have her present informative material to senior leaders instead of himself. Of course, she was nervous about doing so at first, until he instilled in her that, "You know more about this information than they do. You're the expert! I'm just there to walk you into the room." Samantha is by no means shy about the fact that Brian's leadership and influence provided a vehicle to help her get to where she is today.

As I stated earlier, Kurt Grossheim is one of the most recent leaders who influenced me in my current leadership posture. I admittedly stated to Kurt during our interview that I had recently received praise on my verbal delivery from one of my teammates after an all-employee townhall meeting, which I deflected to Kurt. I kindly said, "Thank you," to my teammate, but very quickly followed with the fact that I could not take full credit for the way that I deliver messaging. This employee received a quick lesson on Kurt Grossheim, who works at a completely different organization, and the employee replied, "Thank you for your honesty." It was true. When I had the opportunity to interact with Kurt on a somewhat regular basis, I paid very close attention to how he delivered his verbal messaging at varying levels of audience sizes. I hitchhiked some of my verbal delivery as a leader, and the evidence of success was in the response from this teammate. Interestingly enough, Kurt revealed to me that he did the same thing during his career progression. Hitchhiking is not a shortcut. It is taking the same route, utilizing someone else's vehicle, which they willingly provide.

Creating space

I doubt many people realize that they do this, but we utilize our thumbs hundreds of times per day to create space. How? We do it when typing or texting. If you're like me, and you type 90 words per minute because you're on a computer all day, it may even be more than hundreds of times per day. In leadership, you can use your leadership thumbs to press upon your team, or you can release your thumb off their necks and give them space to operate. Your teams need space to breathe without the threat of their leader's thumb on their necks. This is especially true for leaders who lead leaders.

Leaders who are inexperienced with leading other leaders often make the mistake of smothering their leadership team in an attempt to recreate the success they had when they were in junior leadership positions. A lesson that I learned from my Great Aunt Edna is that no one is you. She said, "Baby, God only had time to make one of you. He spent so much time depositing gifts into your spirit that he almost did not have time to make your sister." (That's funny to me). Of course, everything that my Great Aunt Edna says is true; therefore, if God only had time to make one of me, I cannot expect my leadership team to operate in the exact same manner that I did. They need space to operate within their own gifts.

Recognition

Very much like the convoluted English language, there are identical thumb gestures that mean different things in different situations. One example is the "Thumbs Up," vertical position of the thumb, which can be confused with the same thumb posture as hitchhiking. One version of the posture means, "Can I have a ride?" The other version of the posture means, "Great job! Can I have a ride to Happy Hour to celebrate?" The latter meaning should be utilized regularly by leaders for acknowledging a teammates' ownership of their Accountability. Notice that I did not say recognition for success. As My Great Aunt EDNA mentions, success moments should be celebrated! A niece or nephew of My Great Aunt EDNA should recognize a teammate accepting Accountability with a Thumbs Up act that is noticeable. Although we may assume accountability should be part of one's job responsibilities they automatically accept, real leaders know that this is not always the case. In a cultural environment of My Great Aunt EDNA, teammates accept Accountability because they see their leader doing the same. When you notice this is happening, you know the culture is beginning to take root.

I suggest you all work on the sexiness of your thumbs. People put way too much focus and attention on the middle finger, but the thumbs put in work! Thumbs up!

Broken Mirror

When My Great Aunt EDNA asks for Accountability as a leader, the first step should be to reflect. Reflection should be done in a manner in which the leader temporarily isolates oneself from the situation to assess the viewpoint of organizational impact, cultural impact, team impact, and overall results of the leadership direction provided to the team. To properly reflect, a leader must be able to see themselves. As My Great Aunt EDNA once told me, it is hard to see the frame when you are in the picture. There are two ways in which a leader can properly reflect. One way is to remove yourself from the picture momentarily. The second, is to metaphorically "look in a mirror."

One of the oldest and longest-held possessions I have is a broken mirror. I have owned this broken mirror for thirty-four years. It has been with me on four continents, over a dozen countries, in a war, hospital stays, interview preparations, and life in general. It is only 3" x 3" in size, and the handle was broken off before I was ever given this "gift." I can vividly remember the day I received it as a young Private in the US Army in Ft. Huachuca, AZ in 1988. I needed another mirror to see the back of my head in the primary mirror to cut my own hair. One of my peer female soldiers happily said, "Here, you can have this one. It is broken, but it will work." I doubt she ever imagined this little broken mirror would not only stay with me for the rest of my life, but that it would help me grow as a leader philosophically.

As a leader, we often have a view of who we are as a leader prior to reflection. We will say things to ourselves like, "My team loves me. I am a good people-leader. I understand how people think. I plan well. My boss respects and trusts me. I understand the business." In other words, I know who I am. When leaders do this, they are not surprised by the picture they see of themselves when they reflect. What they do not realize is that they have become the artist and the picture, and they are not really "looking in a mirror." They are reflecting on their own self-portrait. A true view in a mirror will reveal several "new" features a leader may not have been aware of beforehand. You know what I mean, right? "When did this new wrinkle show up?!"

Here is why I love my broken mirror so much. Whenever I look in that mirror, it is large enough for me to see my whole face. But the reflection that I see allows me to see the segmented portions of my face within the cracks. I am constantly reminded that there are segments of me that people see more of than the other segments of my "leadership face." It also shows me portions of my leadership face that has cracks in it. As My Great Aunt EDNA reminds me, Excellence is not Perfection. I never see a "perfect" reflection of myself in my truth mirror. If I happen to hold the mirror on another side and turn it (situational changes), I realize the cracks move. Philosophically, it reminds me that different people have different views of me as a leader, therefore, they see cracks others did not when looking at the same "segment" of my face.

So, how does this help me as a leader when reflecting on my Accountability in situations? When I reflect, I try not to begin with a self-portrait. I begin with an understanding that my leadership face to others will have cracks in it. As stated in another one of My Great Aunt EDNA's leadership lessons, look for the cracks. At this point, the cracks are simply my assumptions during reflection. I later have 1:1 conversations with my leaders, my team, and my peers to gain a full understanding of their assessment. Then, when fully understood, it is time to accept Accountability for successes and challenges and make the necessary adjustments to move towards Excellence.

<u>My high-top fade with the slanted part in the middle was beast back in the day! I could hold my own with the Fresh Prince, Kid 'n Play, and Kwame. My truth mirror may have been cracked, but it got the job done very well.</u>

It Wasn't Me!

Deny, deny, deny! This is the mantra of The Players' Club! All of the real players out there understand where I am coming from! Can I get a whoop-whoop?! If they catch you in the act, or even suspect that you have ill will towards them and have the nerve to confront you, deny, deny, deny! This stance has even made Shaggy a multi-millionaire with his song "It Wasn't Me," and has helped to resurface Mila Kunas and Ashton Kutcher in a Cheetos commercial with the same theme. I have to admit, the song is rather funny, and the commercial memorable, stating the opposite of what was just witnessed with evidence. I would even go as far to say this sad thematic strategy works for leaders in the highest of positions. But My Great Aunt EDNA would never allow me, or her other nieces and nephews, to get away with this approach. She demands Accountability.

So let's say, for hypothetical sake, we had someone in a true position of leadership (maybe even the President of the United States) who blatantly denies any accountability for a violent event that is vividly caught on video and disseminated throughout the entire planet. Should we, as members of the optically and audibly unchallenged population assume the posture that since he/she is in a leadership position, he/she should be excused from accountability? Let me bring this down to everyday situations. Let us assume that you or I have current leaders in our business environment who are abrupt and disrespectful to the team, which has caused high attrition and overworked the employees who remain. Are we to accept their "It wasn't me," mantra and continue as is?

My Great Aunt EDNA teaches that all parties of a team should be held accountable to maintaining a spirit of Excellence in operation, and to their respective areas of team responsibilities. Teams that operate without accountability are referred to as hoodlums, and as my real grandmother and Aunt Edna would tell me when I was young, "Hang around 9 hoodlums long enough and soon enough you will become the 10th." Accountability with My Great Aunt EDNA is real, and leaders who operate within her parameters understand that it includes themselves as well.

One of the best ways to win the confidence of your team as a leader is to state the responsibilities publicly and audibly you will be held accountable for as their leader. Examples can include:

1. I am accountable for ensuring all team members feel valued and respected at all times.

2. I am accountable for helping you get to the next level in your career, whether within this organization or another organization that meets your career criteria.

3. I am accountable to ensure our team always performs with a spirit of excellence, striving for the best possible performance.

Lastly, end with a statement that it is an expectation for all team members to hold the leader accountable when they notice established responsibility expectations are not being met. Some of the best leadership advice can come directly from your team. The last thing they would like to hear from you when they confront accountability shortcomings is, "It wasn't me." Be better. Be excellent. Be strong enough to own your accountability.

I had the great fortune of picking the brain of an exceptional leader who is astute in Accountability. He is a former US Army Officer (Huah!) and a current Vice President of Enercon. Shaun Lott is a Retired Lieutenant Colonel, who is intimately familiar with the importance of Accountability. He explains that during his time serving in the US Army as an officer for over two decades, it was imperative to not only enforce standards, policies, and procedures, but to ensure he exhibited the same through rigorous accountability measures. Doing things any other way would leave the door open for creating double-standards or a, "Do as I say, not as I do" culture.

He recalls being coached by leaders who worked for him to change reports to "not look bad". He asked ,"Why?", and the two leaders said, "Sir, it is no one's business about which soldiers failed. We will make it look good on paper, so you look good as our leader. Plus, we do not bring any unwanted attention to our organization." Shaun replied abruptly, "I am not here to look good! I am here to help the organization get better and achieve our annual objectives. I welcome the scrutiny and accountability brought on by our shortfalls, because it will only make us better! Accountability makes us better!"

Accountability is in fact a two-way street. Most people think employees throughout an organization need to be held accountable, but so do leaders! Accountability throughout all leadership levels is a crucial aspect of corporate governance, as it helps to ensure leaders are acting in the best interests of the organization and its stakeholders, not for self-gain or reverence. It also helps to build trust and confidence in the leadership of the organization, as well as promoting transparency and honesty in decision-making. If an organization lacks trust and confidence in its leadership, the organization is fractured or well on its way to catastrophic failure.

There are several key methods by which leaders can be held accountable for their actions. One way is using performance metrics and targets, which allow leaders to be evaluated against specific goals and objectives. This can include financial metrics, such as profitability and revenue, as well as non-financial metrics, such as customer satisfaction and employee engagement.

Another way accountability can be achieved is using reporting and disclosure requirements. These requirements obligate leaders to provide regular updates on the performance and financial position of the organization, and to disclose any material (good or bad) information that may be relevant to stakeholders. This helps to ensure leaders are transparent and open about the state of the organization, and that stakeholders have access to the information they need to make informed decisions.

Leadership accountability can also be maintained using board oversight. Most organizations have a board of directors or trustees, who are responsible for overseeing the activities of the organization and holding executives to account. This can include reviewing and approving strategic plans and budgets, as well as evaluating the performance of executives against predetermined targets.

In addition to these formal mechanisms, leadership accountability can also be supported using informal processes, such as employee feedback and stakeholder engagement. By regularly soliciting input and feedback from employees and stakeholders, leaders can ensure they are considering the needs and concerns of these groups and can be held accountable for their actions and decisions as well.

Overall, leadership accountability is a crucial aspect of corporate governance, as it helps to ensure leaders are acting in the

BEST interests of the organization and its stakeholders. By using a combination of formal and informal mechanisms, leaders can be held accountable for their actions, and organizations can build trust and confidence in their leadership. Accountability makes us all better!

Still Waters Turn Green

Have you ever owned a swimming pool and the water pump stopped working? This happened to me in the middle of the summer of 1998 in Memphis, TN. If you have never lived in Memphis, TN in July, I am here to let you know that it is excruciatingly hot and humid, and you can honestly begin to question the rationale for life on Earth if you have a lawn to mow. My swimming pool pump malfunction was one of the worst, most costly, and best life lessons that My Great Aunt EDNA reminds me of regularly. I learned a few things that summer. One is water is intended to be perpetually in a state of motion, and if you allow water to remain stagnant in extreme heat, bad things happen. Secondly, green algae loves stagnant swimming pools in suburban Memphis in the summer. Third, so do frogs.

In this metaphorical example, the pump has the accountability of keeping the contents of the pool in motion. In business, leaders are the pumps that are the Accountability My Great Aunt EDNA stresses. When leaders fail to keep things moving in their own work pools, teams become stagnant, grow algae, and eventually invite frogs to join them. Plainly speaking, still waters turn green, and it is very expensive to reinvigorate and purify them again.

There is an existing leadership theory that envisions the role of a leader as someone who makes puzzle pieces fit together. In this theory, it is the leader's responsibility to find the right pieces, determine where they belong, and then place them in those positions to create one team picture. The problem with this theory is that once a picture is complete, it becomes a stagnant image. My Great Aunt EDNA envisions teams as liquid, in a constant state of motion. The leader's role then becomes focused on establishing boundaries (Spirit of Excellence), setting direction (the pump), and then allowing the water to flow uninhibited within those boundaries. If you love looking at water as I do, try to imagine someone micromanaging its movement. It is literally impossible to do. Water can be directed, but its every move cannot be controlled.

When liquid teams have a strong pump, the team remains purer, is not inviting for unwanted pests, and does not create an environment where bacteria and algae grow. The team feels freer to operate within established boundaries, and more external stakeholders desire to partake in the recreation of the team's culture. Being the strong leadership pump for your team requires a leader pulls the team in closely, circulates the team through the system (individual coaching), and then sends the team out strongly (with renewed confidence) back into the environment in a particular direction to re-engage with the team without micromanaging the movement.

If you are a leader who is struggling with stagnation on your team, re-envision how you can be the pump to send your team in a new direction. Sometimes, it is as simple as breaking up the picture you created, establishing new boundaries, and then allowing your team to flow in the direction you establish, in the manner which they desire.

My Inner Thoughts on Writing this Book

As this book comes to a close, I would like to share my personal thoughts on the process of reaching this point of completion of my first book project. As I look back on my life, I now realize the true meaning of "God makes all things good for those who are called according to his purpose." I was called to write this book long before I ever realized it, and He has taken all of the things that have occurred to me in my life, allowed me to view them through the lens of leadership, and tell those stories in a way that people can relate to in their everyday lives and career. I believe the key to me reaching this point is that I eventually accepted the calling that was placed upon me to be a leadership conduit, and now everything I see and do comes back to me in metaphorical versions of what leadership is, could be, and should be. It is the gift of taking the good, the bad, and the ugly, and then finding a way to help other people, and eventually myself.

Clarity was provided to me in a dream as to what else has led me to this point of leadership infatuation. I was reminded in my dream of when I was ten years old and standing in Ft. Huachuca, AZ on a bright sunny afternoon. I was new to the area, and had recently transitioned from four years in Frankfurt, Germany. I stood and made a very slow 360 circle, admiring the peaks of the Cochise Mountains. They were beautiful, but I simultaneously felt a feeling of entrapment. My ten-year-old mind could not conceive how to get out of those mountains without flying over them. My next thought led me the rest of my life. It was, "**I wonder what is on the other side of those mountains?**" I've had many mountains in my leadership career, and I've been able to climb them all and tell the story of the other side. Curiosity was my catapult.

A mountain in my life has never derailed me because I am always wondering what is on the other side of it. Writing a book is a mountain; ask any author. It is a slow climb. You can sometimes see the peak, but at times all you see are the trees in front of you. Ideas come and go, and even if they stick around, you question whether or not the idea would be valid or interesting to the reader. There are obstacles to get around, go over, or go under when climbing a mountain. In book writing, there are fears that show their fangs periodically, which make you question continuation. Those fears include self-doubt, knowledge accuracy, grammatical fluidity, and just plain fear of the book being dead on arrival.

I am filled with intellectual curiosity to see what is on the other side of writing and publishing this book. It is exciting, emotionally enticing, and inspiring for me personally. If the book happens to be dead on arrival, it will have lived a great pre-life in my experience of creating it.

LEADER BIOS:

Ed Brinson, General Manager, American Airlines Destin-Ft. Walton Beach, FL

Ed Brinson is a professional commercial aviation leader with 20+ years of experience working with thousands of employees and leading several different workgroups within the world's largest airline. Ed went directly into the United States Marine Corps out of high school, joining at the age of 17 years old. After 8 years in the USMC, he was honorably discharged and is now a proud US Marine combat veteran of the Desert Storm Era. After the Corps, his secondary educational studies included business administration and he ventured into business for himself.

He later landed his dream job, which could literally take him to higher places with American Airlines Group. Starting in 2002 in Charlotte, NC, he quickly ascended the corporate ladder into management, and he was part of a leadership team, managing thousands of employees and several hundred millions dollars in aviation assets. After working several years in one of the busiest airline hubs in the country, Ed took on a different role as General

Manager of the American Airlines Group operation in Destin-Fort Walton Beach Airport and Panama City, FL Airport.

Throughout his 20+ years in aviation, Ed helped facilitate leadership development training to hundreds of employees and continues to do so to this day. Several of the students in his earlier leadership classes are now leaders managing large workgroups around the network. If you ask Ed, he will tell you that you never stop growing, and that there's always something to learn when it comes to leadership. He strongly believes in President Theodore Roosevelt's quote, "No one cares how much you know, until they know how much you care."

Chris Caines, Vice President Economic & Social Justice, The Community Reinvestment Fund, USA

Previously, Chris was the founding Executive Director of the FIU Miami Urban Future Initiative, an effort to research and map Miami's economic, occupational, creative and technological assets. He is a 2017 Legacy Magazine 40 under 40 South Florida Black Leader of Today and Tomorrow, a 2017 Harvard Business School Young American Leader, and a 2018 McClatchy Miami Herald Influencer. Chris has a Master's in Public Administration from Florida International University and a Bachelors in Psychology and Sociology from Wesleyan University.

Courtnie Coble, Founder & CEO of The Academy of Goal Achievers

Courtnie Coble is the Founder and Chief Executive Officer of The Academy of Goal Achiever's, a nonprofit organization that provides leadership and mentoring programs for high school students – Its mission is to, "develop youth leaders to impact communities, while preparing students and families for post-secondary success."

Her passion for helping others all started while growing up in Anson County, where she learned about the impact of community and family. She moved to Charlotte, North Carolina in 2000 during her sophomore year at East Mecklenburg High School, where she is a proud graduate of the class of 2002.

High School was an integral time in her life, and it wasn't until her senior year she realized she was not properly prepared for the transition from high school to the real world. Like many students, she was asked about her next steps, but no one provided the individual guidance to get her from high school to college. She navigated the admissions process on her own and ultimately graduated from Virginia State University (VSU), where she had the opportunity to become a member of The National Honor Society for Psychology majors and a member of Delta Sigma Theta Sorority, Inc.

After attending VSU and obtaining her Bachelors of Science in Psychology, she started her career making an impact in the social sector. For seven years she helped homeless youth and families as a Crisis Counselor and shortly afterwards, became a Program Manager for a youth in transition program.

Janelle Duray, Executive Vice President and Chief Operating Officer, Job's for America's Graduates

Janelle Duray has over fifteen years of experience in education and workforce development consulting and nonprofit management. She serves as the Executive Vice President and Chief Operating Officer of Jobs for America's Graduates, a national nonprofit that has served 1.5 million youth since its inception 40+ years ago, and currently serves 75,000 youth across 1,500 communities. In her role, Janelle oversees JAG's internal and external efforts and collaborates with national and state public and private sector leaders, to provide critical services to youth and young adults through JAG programming.

Janelle has served many roles at JAG since 2012. In January of 2020, she was named Executive Vice President and subsequently led the organization through the COVID-19 pandemic, making critical investments in technology, student engagement programming, Federal procurement infrastructure, and overall organizational development for the JAG National Office and its national network made of up 39 State Affiliates. Her leadership throughout the pandemic led the Board of Directors to adopt JAG's

Youth Opportunity and Outcomes 2024 Strategic Goals – the most ambitious goals in JAG's history.

Prior to her commitment to JAG, Janelle consulted with leading Fortune 500 companies and national nonprofits, including ADM, HCA, United Way Worldwide, the AARP Foundation, the National Urban League, and more, to grow their fund development, external affairs efforts, and overall strategy.

Janelle received her Masters of Arts in Public Administration from George Mason University's Schar School of Policy and Government and her Bachelors of Arts in Global Studies from the University of Minnesota-Twin Cities.

Throughout her post-secondary education, Janelle held positions at the Association of American Law Schools and former Minnesota Governor Tim Pawlenty's office. Outside of JAG, Janelle enjoys traveling, concerts, good wine, musing about the cosmos, and her first passion, playing piano.

Coach Marcus George, Winningest (American Football) Coach in European History

Marcus George has spent over 45 years as an educator, counselor, teacher and coach. He graduated from Troy University and started his career at the high school level as a teacher and coach. Later, he attended Auburn University where he worked as a graduate assistant with the football program. While at Auburn, he earned a M. Ed in Counselor Education and added a Master's certification in School Administration. After 28 years overseas coaching with the Department of Defense schools, he retired as the winningest football coach in European history. Coach George makes his home in Smiths Station, Alabama.

Kurt Grossheim, President & CEO Global Holdings

Kurt Grossheim joined Global Holdings in December 2021 as President and Chief Executive Officer. Kurt is dedicated to leading the company in its mission to support consumers on their journey back to financial health.

Kurt's extensive career has spanned both domestic and international financial services, including roles in business leadership, banking, operations, client development, business development and integration, risk management, and regulatory affairs.

Most recently, Kurt was EVP and Chief Operating Officer at Synchrony, a Fortune 200 company. Kurt brings deep experience building high-performing, diverse teams, while leading tech-forward, data-driven transformations focused on enabling growth and enhancing customer experience.

Earlier in his career, Kurt worked for GE Capital and served in a wide range of leadership roles across multiple businesses and functional disciplines in the US and internationally. Some of his roles included President and CEO of GE Money Bank, SVP and

General Manager for one of GE Capital's largest credit card portfolios, and CEO of GE Capital Bank in Austria.

Kurt received his B.A. in Business Administration from the University of Notre Dame and is conversationally fluent in German.

When not working, Kurt enjoys spending time with his wife and three children, playing golf, and working out.

Shaun Lott, Vice President, Enercon Global Sales and Marketing, (Ret) LTC, US Army

Shaun served over 24 years in the United States Army, retiring as Lieutenant Colonel in 2016. He held leadership positions from the platoon to battalion levels, as well as executive staff positions. Lott joined Enercon in January 2020 to lead the company's business development efforts within the defense industry. In 2021, Shaun's leadership responsibilities were expanded, and he now oversees Enercon's global sales division, which services over 110 countries. He holds a Master's Degree in Leadership Studies from the University of Texas at El Paso (UTEP).

Samantha Melting, Senior Vice President & Head of Consumer Bank, Synchrony

Samantha Melting is the Head of the Consumer Bank for Synchrony and is responsible for its business strategy, growth, and cross-functional leadership. Her focus and passion are on delivering competitive deposit solutions that help consumers achieve financial wellness through transformative, innovative, and practical approaches.

Samantha has over 28 years in the financial services industry, having managed deposits, investments, credit cards, and secured lending in the consumer, small business, and wealth management spaces. Prior to joining Synchrony, she held several senior leadership positions during her 18+ years at Bank of America. Most recently, she was Senior Vice President of Banking Products and Investment & Retirement Solutions. Her team provided guidance and solutions to help clients achieve their banking, saving, investment and retirement goals, including product management responsibilities across deposits, credit cards, investments and retirement for the Consumer Bank, Merrill Edge, Merrill Lynch, and US Trust businesses. She has also held leadership roles managing checking products, pricing adherence and execution of consumer deposit products, small business credit card acquisitions, portfolio management strategies, predictive modeling, high risk account management, and portfolio management of the automobile and marine lending businesses.

Samantha graduated with honors from Regis University in Denver, Colorado, where she earned a Bachelor of Science degree in Economics with an emphasis on Econometrics and Finance. Samantha is Six Sigma Black Belt certified. She holds a US Patent and a Latino Corporate Directors Association Board Ready Certificate, and held Series 7, 66, and 24 licenses.

Samantha remains committed to diversity and inclusion and holds leadership positions in the Synchrony employee diversity networks for the Women's Network and the Hispanic Network. Additionally, she volunteers in mentoring roles across various organizations, including The Cherie Blair Foundation. Samantha currently sits on the boards of the Consumer Bankers Association, The W Connection, and The America Saves Campaign and serves as a Community Advisor and Woman of Power for Dress for Success Charlotte. She is also an Executive Member of the Latino Corporate Directors Association. She has been featured in various articles, videos and podcasts promoting financial wellness. She resides in Charlotte, NC with her two children.

Nicole Tinson, Founder & CEO HBCU 20x20

Nicole is the Founder and CEO of HBCU 20x20, social enterprise that connects HBCU students and alumni to jobs and internships. Since September 2017, HBCU 20x20 has placed 1,000+ people into job and internship opportunities, while partnering with companies including AT&T, Intel, Accenture, Electronic Arts, PwC, SpaceX, and more.

She is an alumna of Dillard University and Yale University, a member of Delta Sigma Theta Sorority, Inc., and was recently named on the 2020 Forbes 30 Under 30, Social Entrepreneurs List, in addition to making HBCU Buzz's Top 30 Under 30 List, and Dillard University's 40 Under 40 list.

About the Author

Mac McNeil, Leader, Author, & Nephew of Aunt EDNA

Mac McNeil has been a leader in the financial industry for nearly two decades in various leadership roles. He is currently the Senior Vice President of Operations for the Community Reinvestment Fund, USA where he leads Enterprise Operations, which includes Asset Management, Customer Engagement, Data Management & Analytics, Fund Administration, Learning & Development, Loan Servicing Operations, Process Governance, Risk & Controls, Technology/Automation, Underwriting & Closing, and Vendor Relations. He has leadership responsibility for a data architectural and data science team relationship in Chennai, India.

Mac is the author of **My Great Aunt EDNA** weekly newsletter that highlights the leadership topics of Excellence, Doing Things the Right Way, No Shortcuts, and Accountability. He has written a book titled: **My Great Aunt EDNA – The Golden Girl of Leadership**, which illuminates the leadership philosophy he created, along with contributions from other top business leaders.

He began his career with JPMorgan Chase in Arizona in Branch Banking, and spent four years as a 1st Vice President, District Manager in Southern California. He finished in the top 5% of performance in the country and was recognized two consecutive years as a Top Performing District Manager. He accepted a role with Bank of America as a Vice President, Consumer Market Manager in the Los Angeles East Market in 2014, where he managed 13 financial centers in the East San Gabriel area. He was then offered the position of Vice President, Operations Market Manager, where he managed 60 financial centers and finished 2015 #2 in performance in the country and was recognized as Pinnacle Club Performer top 1%. He also managed 27 financial centers in the San Diego North Market.

Mac became Vice President of Operations Optimization for Synchrony, where he was responsible for leading IRA and Trust call center operations, all bank letters and correspondence, as well as lead optimization initiatives for the Consumer Bank, to include robotic process automation, digital transformation, process mapping, and product development with operations in Charlotte, NC, Merriam, KS, Hyderabad, India, and Manila, Philippines.

Mac has a Bachelor's degree in Business Administration from Pfeiffer University, a Master's degree in Business Administration from the University of Phoenix, and Doctorate (ABD) in Management and Organizational Leadership from the University of Phoenix.

Mac spent four years in the U.S. Army as an Intelligence Analyst in Psychological Operations, Special Operations Command (Airborne), and he is a Desert Storm Veteran. He has served on the Board of Directors for Feeding America of Greater Riverside, Inspire Life Skills Training, Inc, The Christian Adoption Service, The Black Professional Group of Bank of America, The Black Organization for Leadership Development for JPMorgan Chase, and The Minority Supplier Development Service. He has been married for 27 years, has four children and one grandchild, and enjoys golf, travel, and being the Captain of his boat in his spare time.

 www.linkedin.com/in/mac-mcneil-397ba7a

 https://www.linkedin.com/company/my-great-aunt-edna/

 https://www.facebook.com/mygreatauntedna

 https://rss.com/podcasts/mygreatauntedna/

 https://www.youtube.com/@mygreatauntedna

 https://www.instagram.com/mygreatauntedna/

THE END
THANK YOU FOR READING!

- Excellence
- Doing Things the Right Way
- No Shortcuts
- Accountability

www.ingramcontent.com/pod-product-compliance
Lightning Source LLC
Chambersburg PA
CBHW062040290426
44109CB00026B/2679